MARGIAD EVANS

CERIDWEN LLOYD-MORGAN

Series Editor
John Powell Ward

seren

seren is the book imprint of
Poetry Wales Press Ltd
Wyndham Street, Bridgend, Wales

ISBN 1-85411-219-8 hbk
1-85411-220-1 pbk

A CIP record for this title is available from the British Library

*The publisher acknowledges the financial support of the
Arts Council of Wales*

Printed in Palatino
by WBC Book Manufacturers, Bridgend

Contents

List of Illustrations

One
The Immortal Hospital: Memories of Childhood (1909-1929)

The first time I saw the river Wye, at nine years old, I had to be dragged away in endless tears at leaving it.
(Letter to Bryher, 1 November 1949)

They kept asking me what I was crying for; I couldn't tell them for I didn't know – at least I did in a way.
(Letter to Michael Williams, 3 September 1943)

By the 1940s, looking back on her nine-year-old self, Margiad Evans could recognize the importance of her first encounter with Herefordshire and the southern borderland which was to become a source of joy, consolation and inspiration to her until her death of a brain tumour on her forty-ninth birthday. So central was that country to her literary work that one might easily assume that she was born there. She was in fact born at Uxbridge on 17 March 1909, and christened Peggy Eileen Whistler. She was the second daughter of Godfrey James Whistler, then a forty-three-year-old clerk with the Sun Life Assurance Society in London, and his wife Katherine Isabel Wood. The Whistler family had its roots in Buckinghamshire and Oxfordshire, the Woods in Yorkshire, though Margiad Evans noted with pride that her mother had some Irish blood and that she herself was born on St Patrick's Day. It was her paternal grandmother, Ann Evans (1800-79), daughter of a Lancashire clergyman, but believed to be of Welsh extraction, who was to provide the surname for Peggy Whistler's pen-name.

Peggy was one of four children. Her elder sister, Betty, was born in 1907, Nancy followed three and a half years after Peggy in 1912 and finally the only brother, Roger, was born in 1916. By now the family had moved to Gerrards Cross, still very much a rural suburb at that time: 'there were farms then among the villas ... and bracken and holly', she later recalled in her journal (5 November 1946). Two years later, however, in September 1918, the Whistler children faced a major upheaval in their lives when their father resigned his job because of ill-health, perhaps not unconnected with alcohol. This meant that for a couple of years the family had no permanent home, and it may be that uncertainty about their future, and a consequent longing for a stable base, contributed to Peggy's unwillingness to turn her back on Herefordshire after her first visit there with her father. His sister Annie and her husband, Douglas Lane, had settled with their children at a farm called Benhall, a few miles up river from Ross-on-Wye, and Godfrey Whistler took Peggy there for a weekend not long after he had stopped working. On the last day of their visit he took her out for a walk by the river Wye. Her sight of the river that day was to prove momentous, for it was then that she felt what she later called her 'premonition of passion' for the Herefordshire countryside and was reduced to inarticulate tears:

> After some moments he turned away, expecting me to follow him. I did not. He called. I still looked at the river, and some powerful emotion began to rise in me, some desperate adoration. He called again. I turned away and followed him, but when he looked down ... he saw me in a passion of tears. With consternation he stooped, coaxed. What was the matter? All I could sob was: 'Oh don't, don't take me away from this place.'
> ('The Immortal Hospital')

Her distress as a child at being separated from it also foreshadows a deeper, more consciously understood grief in her later years, when, in the autumn of 1953, she had to leave the Border Country and move to Sussex, to spend her last years in exile there.

In March 1920, two years after her first brief visit to Herefordshire, Peggy, then just coming up to her eleventh birthday, returned to her aunt's house. At this time the Whistlers had no permanent home of their own, and while the parents stayed with relatives, the eldest daughter was sent to boarding school. But Peggy, together with her younger sister, Nancy, then aged seven, spent a whole year at Benhall. This period spent together on the farm seems to have forged their close relationship. Perhaps partly because their cousins were older than them, too old to play with them, the two girls became inseparable, despite the gap of three years between them. Their relationship at times seemed like that of twins, although they were very different personalities, as the writer later recalled. Nancy, later renamed Sian by Peggy, was more extrovert, active and daring than the more contemplative Peggy, and Nancy 'caught nuances of behaviour which escaped me, engrossed as I was in the odours and suggestions of *place*'. It was Peggy, not Nancy, who loved to sit for hours reading the old books she found in the house – R.M. Ballantyne's *The Dog Crusoe*, J.W. Fortescue's *The Story of a Wild Deer*, Harriet Beecher Stowe's *Uncle Tom's Cabin* and *The Wide, Wide World* by Elizabeth Wetherell – until Nancy's insistent voice called her away to adventures outdoors. Margiad was called 'dreamy' because 'I liked to read and write and make up stories about places and our cousins' old dolls'. Nevertheless, 'Sian [Nancy] and myself so different, yet so closely bound, were identical in our harmony with natural time and natural laws'. Often there was very little talk between them, for 'our converse was in the things we did together'. The year they spent together at Benhall without their parents later came to represent for Peggy a golden age, a lost world of innocent, irresponsible childhood. But it also provided a store of vivid impressions and memories which were to inform her writing throughout her life. 'Everything happened to me when I was a child', she wrote in 1943 in the conclusion of *Autobiography*, 'and though all vestiges of my childhood are gone out of the world, what was deepest in me then is my depth still'. As we shall see, images of Benhall, Aunt Annie and other characters associated with that period constantly reappear throughout her work. When reflecting on her childhood, she had in mind a fairly short period, however, up to the age of thirteen, when she began to mature physically. Until then, 'how vivid and pure were the things I saw', she later recalled in *Autobiography*.

The Benhall days provided more than a useful stock of material for the writer to draw on. They also became a source of consolation in her last years when she was increasingly disabled. In 'The Immortal Hospital', the unpublished account of her childhood which she wrote in 1957, she argued that memories of childhood, which are always inside us, could be a 'refuge for joy' and their immense healing powers could be drawn on in later life. A stay in that 'immortal hospital for every kind of misery, physical and mental', could be powerfully therapeutic.

At the end of their long stay at Benhall Peggy and Nancy were reunited with the rest of the family. The Whistlers had bought a house called Lavender Cottage at Bridstow, just west of Ross across the River Wye, inland from Benhall but within easy walking distance of the farm. Even today, despite the sound of traffic on the bypass barely half a mile away, Bridstow is a quiet, scattered rural settlement. Leaving the main road, the lane passes on the right the church of St Bridget, which gives the parish its name. It was substantially rebuilt in the nineteenth century but its fourteenth-century tower is more or less intact. Across the road, in the new cemetery, lies the grave of Godfrey James Whistler, and a few hundred yards further on, just after a turn off to the left, Lavender Cottage still stands. This was the home of the Whistler family until 1936, a firm base to which Peggy constantly returned.

The High School in Ross which she attended was little more than a large house, despite its name, and the education she received there was of the kind considered suitable for a girl at that time, with the emphasis on literature, art, music and sewing, rather than maths and science. Miss Mabel Morling, who taught French at the school, made a particular impression on her. Miss Morling, who became friendly with Mrs Whistler and was a frequent visitor to Lavender Cottage, later remembered Peggy as a high-spirited, clever and interesting pupil, good at English and art. She passed her Oxford Junior exam in 1923 and gained her School Certificate two years later. Like her mother, Peggy was musically gifted, had a fine singing voice and played the piano and violin. As she grew up she become shortsighted and had to wear glasses. 'How would you like me in big goggledy glasses?' she wrote to her brother in September 1924. 'When you come home you will see me wearing them. They make me look very stern'. Despite her success at school, she did not stay on after gaining her School Certificate. Further study at a university was apparently not considered, but it would have been unusual for a Ross girl in those days to take a degree. Instead she left home and went to spend a few months teaching and studying at a school in France, but this was equally unusual and a bold step to take. Even at that age she must have had great determination and a strong sense of purpose. She was to need those qualities to cope with the trying circumstances that lay before her at the school, the Cours Saint-Denis. The school was in Loches, a picturesque town some twenty miles south-west of Tours, its houses huddled together at the foot of a rocky hill topped by a mediaeval castle, 'a place to look at but not to live in' (*The Wooden Doctor*, 39). The Cours Saint-Denis stood at the end of a quiet street, on the very edge of the town.

Loches and the school, renamed Laroche and the Cours Saint-Louis, dominate the first section of her heavily autobiographical second novel, *The Wooden Doctor* (1933). In view of her known enthusiasm for the work of the Brontë sisters, it is possible that reading Charlotte Brontë influenced her literary treatment of the school, but there can be no doubt that the fictional account was firmly based on her own experience in France. The school's spartan regime and strict, petty discipline shocked her and made her time there an extremely hard and unhappy one. A letter to her brother Roger, written from Loches in early December 1925, is not self-pitying, but it more than hints at her misery and the difficulties she encountered. Everyone had colds, but in bed in the dormitories they were not allowed to cough or sneeze. She was teaching little boys of about five years of age, 'very lazy, very naughty, very ignorant and always crying like little girls ... This afternoon I shall teach them drawing. It is very difficult to teach people to count in French when you often forget yourself'.

The reference to teaching drawing is significant, for although she would later concentrate on her writing, in her teens she felt more drawn towards art. The family's distant connection with James McNeill Whistler had made an impression on her. In later life she boasted to the American writer Bryher that she was a Whistler 'and all Whistlers have an *idea* of art'. She recalled in 'The Immortal Hospital' that a picture which hung in her aunt's bedroom at

Benhall had been painted by her grandfather, Henry Ratcliffe Whistler, in the company of the famous artist. It was as an illustrator that her publisher, Basil Blackwell, first knew her, and throughout her career her drawing and painting continued to be extremely important to her. Her first book, *Country Dance*, and her one published collection of short stories, *The Old and the Young*, were both illustrated by her; she designed dust-jackets and frontispiece illustrations for *The Wooden Doctor* and *Creed*, and even in her declining years she drew greetings cards and pictures in ink, watercolour or pastels for relatives and friends. Although it was as a writer that she would make her name in the long term, when she left Loches and returned home to Bridstow it was art, not writing, that attracted her most. A chance encounter with the work of Aubrey Beardsley had made a great impression on her and she had apparently experimented with line-drawings. Eventually, in 1926, it was agreed that she should attend classes at the Hereford School of Art, where she concentrated on studying etching. She used to travel there and back by bicycle once a week, a round trip of about thirty miles. Even after completing the course, she continued to bring work in for criticism from her tutor.

Although this training was rather limited, she felt confident in her ability as an artist, and somehow managed to persuade her parents to let her spend a few months in Brittany in 1926, at Pouldu in Finistère. Her decision to undertake this stay abroad on her own shows remarkable confidence for a girl still in her teens, but perhaps after her stay at the Cours Saint-Denis she felt that nothing again could be so bad. If nothing else, that experience had probably given her greater confidence, as well as fluency in spoken French, and she may well have grown almost unconsciously to appreciate certain aspects of French life and culture despite her miserable life at the school. It is also possible that, having hitherto been part of a large family, she relished the prospect of time on her own, to organize her day as she wished. There is no doubt that throughout her life she could enjoy even protracted periods of solitude without feeling lonely, although she was by no means anti-social. As her writing career developed, of course, she needed peace and quiet on her own, and at times that was not easy to obtain. Without clear periods of solitude she wrote less and with greater difficulty, for example in the late 1930s.

During her late teens Peggy was already keeping a regular journal, and apparently drew on this source very heavily when she came to write *The Wooden Doctor* in 1932. Although it does not appear in the published version, a long section based on her stay at Pouldu is included in the surviving manuscript draft of the novel. Pouldu (the black pool) is a fishing village south of Quimperlé, at the mouth of the river Laïta. Like Pont-Aven, which lies a few miles north-west, it was then a popular resort for artists. The village was divided into two, later described in the draft of *The Wooden Doctor*:

> Haut Pouldu was modern, given over to tourists and summer visitors. It had villas, shops that sold lace and antique Breton furniture, a hard white road leading to the Grande Plage ... But Bas Pouldu was old and smelt of bait. The antique furniture was used in the homes of the fisher folk.

It was in Bas Pouldu that she stayed. The village was 'entirely Breton':

> ... men went in jeans of faded blue ... women in black full skirts. On Sundays and fête days they were very gorgeously attired in silks, velvets and brocades with embroidered aprons, stately ruffs and coifs decorated with pink or blue ribbons. A man and all his children might hide behind his wife's petticoats.

She put up at an *auberge* favoured by artists, 'barely fifty yards from the water's edge'. It was still quiet when she arrived in early May, because the season had not yet begun. This was to be a formative visit in more ways than one. Not only did she make lifelong friendships, notably with Nell, a sophisticated but superstitious Parisienne, and Georges, a young man of Polish descent, but the vivid impressions she formed of life in the local fishing community never left her. Although they are not directly reflected in any of her published work, she retained strongly visual memories of them. They returned to her vividly during the Second World War, prompted by descriptions of small towns in the Mediterranean in letters from her husband in the Navy. In one letter she described how 'when there was a Pardon they used to sew roses on sheets and hang them out over the house, like arras. And between white walls the black-dressed people processed, looking shiny and muscular' (9 March 1945). She remembered too 'the fishing boats with their sandstone sails and blue muslin nets drying from the masts', the harbour at Concarneau 'full of their chiffon folds' (29 March 1945).

These recollections, and the adapted journal account in the draft version of *The Wooden Doctor*, indicate that her stay in Brittany was a happy one. She enjoyed considerable freedom for a young girl on her own, but had the security of the homely atmosphere of the *auberge* and the informality of life with other artists. In some ways, although it does not so obviously impinge on her published work, her stay at Pouldu takes on a similar quality to the year spent with Nancy at Benhall with Aunt Annie Lane. It was undoubtedly a period of happiness and freedom, combining much time spent outdoors and a homely house with good food and comfort. 'Brittany I have kept', she told her husband (31 March 1945); it was a treasure to value, perhaps even another part of the 'immortal hospital'.

After her return her life remained rather peripatetic for a few years. Although Lavender Cottage still provided a strong anchor, she spent periods away from home on her own, but now she was earning her own money. One autumn she went to work as a governess for a family of Syrian descent called Gadban, who lived at Alton in Hampshire. The three sisters were away at boarding school, but Peggy taught their younger brother Paul, who was about five or six years old at the time. He retained few precise impressions of her but more than thirty years later still remembered how she used to read to him Tennyson's 'The Lady of Shalott'. Even after twenty years had passed, late autumn days would remind Peggy of the mood of this time and she used to refer in her journals to the arrival of 'the Gadban season'.

Another temporary post, but one which was to have long-term consequences, took her to Oxford. There she became housekeeper to Miss Margaret Lucy Lee (1871-1955), founder and headmistress of the Wychwood School in the Banbury Road. She was an Anglo-Saxon specialist, and a Home Tutor at the University, teaching women of the Society for Home Students which was later to become

St Anne's College. Miss Lee made a great impression on Peggy, who described her with great affection in a letter to her American friend Bryher in May 1952:

> She ... was very good to me and used to call me one of her students though I was only with her to housekeep and answer the telephone ... At seventy if no-one were about – or if she thought they weren't – she'd slide down the bannisters. She had a face like a naughty boy of twelve. I loved her and she used to tell me about ODES and all that. The worst driver in Oxford.

Their affection was mutual, as was their appreciation of each other's eccentricities. Writing to Peggy in March 1948, Miss Lee began her letter 'Yes, quite mad, but then you always were, and wouldn't be my Peggy if sane.' Despite her taste for periods of solitude, Peggy enjoyed company if it was congenial, and age and differences of background were unimportant to her: what mattered was that the individual should have spirit and interest her.

It may have been through the remarkable Miss Lee that Peggy first met Basil Blackwell, the publisher and bookseller whose shop still dominates the lower end of Broad Street in Oxford. This meeting was to have two important results: her friendship with Blackwell's daughter Helen, and her first commission. At this stage Peggy, despite keeping a journal, still regarded herself primarily as an artist, and was pleased to be invited by Basil Blackwell to provide a series of illustrations for a book he was publishing. This was a collection of Eastern tales called *Tales from the Panchatantra*, translated and retold by the self-taught Sanskrit scholar, Alfred Williams (1877–1930), a poet, folk-song collector and former steamhammer man at the Great Western Railway locomotive factory in Swindon. Peggy, who was still only twenty years old, was commissioned to make thirty pen and ink drawings, work that suited her perfectly since both inclination and training had led her to this type of monochrome work. Eighteen of the original drawings survive, still betraying slight traces of her teenage enthusiasm for Beardsley, but completely appropriate for the fairy-tale narratives they were designed to illustrate, and in the finished volume text and pictures are perfectly married. She also designed the dust-jacket, with a semi-abstract decoration, again with a suitably Eastern mood. Since Alfred Williams died shortly after Blackwell agreed to publish the tales, Peggy had no opportunity to discuss the work with him and had to rely on her own response to the texts.

Although her career as an illustrator of other people's work was short-lived, this commission was a valuable experience, for she began to learn about the process of printing and publishing. It also taught her the importance of self-discipline in producing the work required according to specifications and within a given time limit. But above all to see her work in its published form must have given her considerable satisfaction and boosted her confidence in her ability. Blackwell's evident approval of her finished work was important to her too, for she soon became greatly attached to him, seeing him as a kind of father figure.

Her work for the *Tales from the Panchatantra*, published in 1930, may not have led to much further work as an illustrator, but it can be seen, in retrospect, as an important step in her career, for it inspired her to write and illustrate a story in a similar style. As its title suggests, 'A Fairy Story' is heavily influenced by the Eastern tales of the *Panchatantra*, both with regard to the narrative and the black and white drawings and decoration with which she adorned the surviving fair copy. This manuscript, signed 'PW', remained unpublished at her death. It must have been produced about 1930, shortly after she finished the *Panchatantra* drawings. The story, set in a vaguely exotic setting, tells of an old man called Shanlea who makes birdcages in a land without birds. The king learns from him that Shanlea was heir to a kingdom where birds lived and sang, but had preferred studying to ruling his country and so was deposed. The king and Shanlea finally reach the kingdom, but the king prevents Shanlea from caging the golden bird which would enable him to fulfil the condition for him to regain his kingdom. Finally Shanlea dies, but the golden bird is found in the cage with the old man: 'he had come into his inheritance'.

'A Fairy Story' is a work of apprenticeship, derivative and uneven in style , but nevertheless it has great assurance as well as charm, and shows Peggy's ability to bring together successfully the visual and verbal aspects of her imagination. It can also be seen as a work of transition, for from now onwards, although she would never completely neglect her drawing and painting, she concentrated increasingly on her writing as a means of expression, even if she often wrote with an artist's eye. It was also the first and last time she signed her written work as Peggy Whistler.

Two
The Birth of Margiad Evans
(1930-32)

Her twentieth year proved to be a turning point for Peggy Whistler. Not only did she achieve her first commission as an illustrator, she also began to conceive the idea for her first novel. She had spent some time at the home of her cousin, Dorothea Churchill-Longman, who lived at Swinbrook Manor not far from Burford in Oxfordshire. Dorothea's husband wrote novels under the pen-name of Spencer Watts, and after her work on the *Panchatantra* Peggy was commissioned to design the jacket of his first published novel, a love story entitled *Yesterday's Tomorrow*, which appeared in 1931. It may be that this contact with a novelist encouraged Peggy to consider trying her own hand as a writer. The third part of her second book, *The Wooden Doctor*, contains an imaginative account of her stay at Swinbrook, where the narrator, Arabella, based on Peggy Whistler, helps to look after the children. If this literary reconstruction of her visit to Swinbrook Manor is to be believed, Peggy-Arabella had been encouraged to write by her headmistress, but had hitherto had little confidence in her ability. She had tried two years previously to write a story of her own, but had not managed to complete it to her satisfaction. Now she took out the manuscript she had brought with her and began to work on it again, partly in an attempt to cope with her low spirits. This time she found greater success and pleasure in her writing:

> I wrote for my distraction, using as a background the country-
> side in which I had grown up: my characters I had known since

18

childhood. Gradually my creations, these puppets with a strange wilful life of their own, took complete possession of my imagination. I could not tell where truth ended and fiction began; I discovered what a pleasure I could find in blending the two.

(*The Wooden Doctor*, 151)

As the work progresses Arabella feels 'a new power flow through my mind' (p. 151) and becomes exultant at her own power: 'I felt a strange excitement; the conviction swept over me that what I had written was good, better than I had ever done before' (p. 153).

A visit to another cousin marks another step in her progress, the conception of her first novel, *Country Dance*, which was published in 1932. In late July 1929 Kitty, the youngest daughter of Peggy's aunt Annie Lane of Benhall, got married and went to live near Monmouth, only about ten miles south-west of Bridstow. Peggy went to stay with Kitty very soon afterwards, and during her visit came across the precise setting for her first novel. Kitty Meredith later recalled how they went for long walks together and 'on one occasion we found an empty tumbledown cottage on top of the "Buckholt" (a wooded hill just outside Monmouth) where the view was magnificent. We sat on the stone seat of the porch and made up stories about the lives of the people who had lived there. Peggy told me later it was here the idea of her *Country Dance* was born'. This is undoubtedly the place described so exactly in the introduction to the story:

> The shepherd's cottage where Ann was born is falling to ruin on top of the hill. I wish it were not so far gone, that the garden where she worked were not overrun with weeds. The garden walls have vanished, sheep crop around the doorstep, and only the two stone benches remain as they were when she was alive. The chimneys have fallen, the wind and rain make free with the windows, inside it is not safe to tread the narrow staircase, and the fireplaces are choked with fallen plaster.
>
> (*Country Dance*, viii)

Kitty Meredith's testimony, together with Peggy's own references to her childhood practice of 'mak[ing] up stories about places', provide an important key to our understanding of all her fiction, for they reveal the importance of a concrete location as a starting point. She had to be able to visualize clearly the place where her characters lived, and feel the atmosphere of that place. Setting aside those characters derived from herself, notably the Arabella of *The Wooden Doctor*, the people in her novels are inextricably linked to their physical and social environment and to imagine them as individuals she had first to have a precise mental image of their home. Most of the places mentioned in her fiction were based on ones she knew well in her formative years and are easily recognizable even though the names have been changed: Salus is obviously Ross, Chepsford is Hereford, Benhall becomes Ell Hall or Hill Hall and so on. The process of locating characters or events in actual places continued later in her career. In the 1940s she mentions Langstone Park, near her home in Llangarron, as the setting for part of her unfinished novel, 'The Widower's Tale'. 'I've been waiting to breathe into me just such a house in its *guilty* place. But it is sad rather than sinister', she wrote to her husband in 1945. Two years later she noted in her diary: 'It never seems inhabited but haunted by an *invisible* decay'. Seeing a house and imagining the life that had once existed there never failed to awake the creative impulse in her: 'Altogether I felt *creative* which to me is to feel things assembling themselves in me'. Without a location, then, there could be no narrative, and the setting could be as important a protagonist as the characters themselves. In the case of *Country Dance* it was the cottage near Monmouth which provided the necessary catalyst for the story to 'assemble itself' in her mind.

Country Dance was important to her as her first literary publication but it also marks her invention of herself as a writer in the full sense of the word. She called that writer Margiad Evans. The choice of the surname was simple, provided, as we have seen, by her grandmother Ann Evans. Margiad, a Welsh form of Margaret, has caused some confusion. In 1952 she confided to the eminent Welsh writer Kate Roberts, that her Pembrokeshire-born, Welsh-speaking father-in-law had always told her that there was 'no such name', that it was 'Marged' and that she had misspelt it for years. Kate Roberts, who was brought up in Caernarfonshire, used the name 'Margiad' in some of her own stories, for that was the form in her home area and neither more nor less valid than 'Marged'. This suggests that it was in Caernarfonshire that Peggy Whistler first heard the name, which is the Welsh equivalent of the English Peggy or Margaret, and chose it for herself. In this case her choice of the name must be linked to her visit in the summer of 1930 to Pontllyfni in Caernarfonshire, where she worked hard at the manuscript of *Country Dance*. This was her most significant visit to Wales, for during her stay she learned and achieved a great deal.

Pontllyfni, which is only a few miles from Rhosgadfan, where Kate Roberts was brought up, is a small village near the sea about eight miles south-west of Caernarfon, the settlement being clustered around the main road from Caernarfon to Pwllheli. It lies on the edge of what was then the major quarrying district of Dyffryn Nantlle. Peggy spent five or six weeks there, as a paying guest at a farm called Coch-y-bûg, inland of the main village and higher up, at the foot of a mountain called Y Foel. The farm was the home of the Lloyd Jones family. Peggy had probably responded to an advertisement offering rooms to let during the summer. Mrs Lloyd Jones, who appears as Mrs Lloyd Owen in *The Wooden Doctor*, died in 1961, but when her son and two daughters were contacted a few years later by Margiad Evans's would-be biographer Arnold Thorpe, they well remembered the young woman who had spent the summer with them more than thirty years previously. Their visitor's lack of concern about her appearance had made a strong impression on Minnie, one of the daughters, though she did add that for special occasions Peggy always had a suitable dress to wear. The young people may have considered it unusual that a girl so close to them in age should come alone to spend a holiday so far away from home. She was not entirely alone, however, for she brought with her her shaggy-haired little dog Griselda. Peggy was a great dog-lover and became extremely attached to Griselda and her successors. Her interest in dogs led her hosts to invite her one day to join them when they went to watch sheepdog trials, an outing which provided her with the material for the sheepdog trials described in *Country Dance* (and probably anachronistic in that context). The Lloyd Joneses were impressed by her observation and careful questioning. She was determined to understand every detail, not only of the trials but also of every aspect of life in the countryside. She must have been struck by the contrast between farming in the lush acres of Benhall, on the banks of the River Wye, and the far harsher life of the Caernarfonshire farmer. Although life in lowland Pontllyfni was easier than for the hill farmers further inland, even so the soil is thin, stony and poor. As in many of the quarrying districts of north-west Wales, those with the smaller agricultural holdings often had to combine farming with waged work in the slate industry in order to make ends meet.

There was also a language difference, for Dyffryn Nantlle was, and still is, a stronghold of Welsh. When Peggy Whistler arrived there she would have heard very little English, and many of the people she met, especially the oldest and youngest, were monoglot Welsh speakers, including the little boy who used to be sent to tell her that dinner was ready. It is striking that in *The Wooden Doctor* she remarks how well the Lloyd Owen girls spoke English, emphasising that this was not their first language nor one that they would use very often. She never acquired enough Welsh to speak it herself, and what Welsh she did learn here she forgot later for lack of practice, but, as she told Kate Roberts in 1946: 'I have never forgotten the fact that thousands of men and women and little children speak nothing else'. Her reaction to the ubiquity of the Welsh language and to her own marginalization by it is strikingly positive, and thus unusual in an English visitor. By now, of course, she had had plenty of experience of being a newcomer, an outsider, an exile even, after so many periods spent away from home without any of her immediate family, and she must have become very self-sufficient. She also had plenty to occupy her during her stay, and there was some English-speaking company at the farm. But she was probably better prepared for Welsh Wales than were most English summer visitors because of the time she had spent in Brittany. Although no census has ever been taken to establish the number of Breton speakers, the language was certainly very much alive in the area of Pouldu and Concarneau in the 1920s, especially among fishermen and old people, so she would already have experienced a similar situation. Since Welsh and Breton are fairly closely related, belonging to the same branch of the family of Celtic languages, she may even have recognized some of the commoner words.

She could hardly have chosen a better place than Pontllyfni to learn something of the language, history and culture of north-west Wales. It is an area closely associated with the mediaeval prose tales known as the Four Branches of the Mabinogi. Many of the place-names, including names of modern farms, appear in those mediaeval texts and the characters and events of the Mabinogi are inextricably linked with Dyffryn Nantlle. Mrs Lloyd Jones was well versed in such stories, as well as more recent ones, and she was delighted to have an appreciative listener. Pontllyfni had also become the home of Ifor Williams, Professor of Welsh at the University College of North Wales in Bangor, and an expert on Old and Middle Welsh. His scholarly edition of the Four Branches of the Mabinogi was published in the year of Peggy's visit. In this Welsh-speaking community, where English class divisions did not apply, a university professor was respected but not regarded as unapproachable. Ifor Williams, moreover, was himself extremely proud of his own humble origins in a similar quarrying district near Bethesda; he felt at ease with working people and greatly relished his conversations with them. It was probably Mrs Lloyd Jones who suggested that Peggy went down the road and knocked on his door to ask for more information than she herself could give.

Myfanwy Williams, the professor's wife, invited her in and gave her some tea while they talked. The visit must have been a success on both sides for it was repeated several times and in a letter to Arnold Thorpe written in 1963 Myfanwy Williams remembered the young writer clearly and with warmth. It was in Pontllyfni that Peggy picked up many of the place-names, such as Craig-y-ddinas and Llyn-tro, which she uses in *Country Dance*, transposing them many miles south-east to the Border country. It was also during her stay at Coch-y-bûg that she learned scraps of traditional Welsh verses and songs which she included in the novel, together with a number of common Welsh phrases in the dialogue. All these she sent to Ifor Williams for checking before submitting her manuscript, showing a respect for the language as well as a concern for accuracy, although a few slips remain.

During her stay in Pontllyfni *Country Dance* seems to have come together in its final form. For Peggy as for Arabella in *The Wooden*

Doctor, the virtual completion of the novel coincided with the end of the summer and of her stay in Wales. It is likely, however, that she spent some time correcting and revising this draft after her return to Bridstow. Eventually she submitted it to the publisher Arthur Barker, who agreed to publish it, and *Country Dance* by Margiad Evans appeared in 1932, dedicated to her mother.

Wherever she went during her stay at Coch-y-bûg, Minnie Lloyd Jones later recalled, Peggy always took with her a sketch-book and drawing materials, proof that writing had not displaced her love of drawing, although over the next few years the writing would come first. When *Country Dance* appeared it included four illustrations 'by Peggy Whistler' and one wonders how many of her readers realized that both writer and artist were the same woman. Her decision to separate the two aspects of her creativity, the written word and visual image, without disturbing their symbiotic relationship, marks a new departure, but also an early sign of an awareness of a duality within her temperament, later to become more pronounced and less comfortable. These new illustrations are also very different from her previous work. Instead of monochrome line-drawings, full of precise details, we find the complete opposite: full colour illustrations without any outlining. Against a plain, greenish background the figures, whose features are left blank or suggested only by a single eye, are made up of flat blocks of colour occasionally dotted with a simple suggestion of patterning of dress or jacket. Deliberately simple, like figures cut out in paper and pasted on to their coloured ground they stand on or move over an invisible floor, which forms one continuous flat plane with their surroundings. Like figures in the country dance of the book's title, they make their formal steps, moving in their pre-ordained pattern, their feet touching no firm ground, creating a dream-like atmosphere. Yet the strong, simple shapes have an almost sculptural quality. Like the narrative of *Country Dance*, they depend on contrasts and symmetries, on patterning with a strong undertow of tension.

This first short novel by Margiad Evans is a remarkable feat. On the surface it seems simple in both structure and plot. The narrative, set in the Border countryside in 1850, consists of the supposed diary of Ann Goodman, divided into two parts, the first leading up to the death of her mother and the second recounting the events of the following few months. The diary itself is framed by a short introduction and conclusion by the author. The introduction, signed by 'Margiad Evans', provides the setting, presenting and justifying the device of the diary. The conclusion recounts the events which took place after Ann's own narrative breaks off, and reflects on the significance of her story, reminding the reader of the themes mentioned in the introduction and bringing the book full circle, just as country dancers, after crossing in ritual movements from one side and one end of the set to the other, return finally to their original positions.

The central character, Ann Goodman, the daughter of a Welsh mother and English father, and living mainly on the English side of the Border, is torn between the contradictory demands made on her by her mixed blood. At the beginning of her story she is expected to marry the Englishman Gabriel Ford, but soon she is courted by the Welshman, Evan ap Evans, who employs her father as a shepherd. The narrative follows Gabriel's increasing jealousy, as he reads in the notebook he has given her of Evan's attentions. The two rivals dance around each other, constantly changing places, but while Gabriel becomes less loving and more violent towards Ann, Evan's behaviour becomes less bullying as he tries to win her. Gradually the tension between the three main protagonists increases, paralleled in the build-up of violence, at first threatened and feared, then bursting out in fights between the two men before culminating in the murder of Ann shortly after she agrees to marry the Welshman. The pull between the two sides is represented not only by her two lovers but also in the rhythm of the relationship between herself and her parents. The narrative opens with Ann going to look after her ailing Welsh mother, which is how she first meets her English father's master Evan ap Evans. After her mother's death she attempts to retreat into neutrality but is drawn back to the Welshman's farm when her father, who becomes a helpless drunkard after he is widowed, needs her help if he is not to lose his work as a shepherd.

The novel is constructed with almost mathematical precision. The narrative moves like a pendulum across the Border, between Wales and England, two contrasting languages, Welsh and English, church and chapel, father's people and mother's people. Ann, whose mixed blood prevents her from fully belonging to one group or the other, stands at the crossover point. The Border itself, like Ann, is represented as an unresolved mixture where Welsh and English cohabit uneasily. Social events are attended by families with both Welsh and English names, which do not necessarily tally with their homes. Mary Maddocks, for example, with whom Ann lives for fourteen years before her mother's last illness, is a cousin of Ann's Welsh mother but speaks English and dislikes her Welsh neighbours; she lives in Wales but her farm, Twelve Poplars, has an English name. The Welshman Evan ap Evans, on the other hand, lives on the English side of the border, near Salus (Ross).

In Ann these contradictions are concentrated. She crosses not only the geographical Border but also social and linguistic boundaries, for she is one of the few characters completely fluent in both Welsh and English, translating for her father when her mother loses her English on her deathbed. Furthermore, she strives to live and work peacefully in communities either side of the Border. She is even at times a link between the domains of women and men, not only because of her relationship with Gabriel and with Evan, which draws her into the ambit of their violent antipathy, but also because when her father is incapacitated and unmanned by his wife's death, she is able to take over his shepherding work in the masculine sphere, despite his earlier rejection of her once her mother had died. In the end she knows too much of all these opposed worlds and cannot survive.

The control of the novel's symmetries and patterning, contrasting with the unfettered emotions and actions it recounts, creates a tension which serves to underline the conflict and violence. Together with the unadorned and understated style of Ann's diary, this makes the events, and Ann's inability to change the movement towards their inevitable conclusion, seem all the more shocking. The use of imagery to suggest this inexorable progress is also carefully paced. Just before the meeting when Gabriel becomes aware of Evan ap Evans's interest in her, Ann sees in her own reflection in the stream what we later discover to be a premonition of her death:

> There is my face staring back at me out of the brown water among the weeds, almost like a person drowned.
> (*Country Dance*, 17)

This is echoed in the brief account of the discovery of her murder: '... the deep pool where Ann was found, her body wrapped in water weeds, her head no more than an inch or two from the surface' (p. 94). Images of water constantly recur between these first and last points: the drowning of the sexton in the floods (p. 8), the pool where the sheep are dipped, with its water 'shallow and dirty, but in the middle ... still and very deep' (p. 19), and the near drowning of Georgie in Llyn-tro with its 'quiet black water, that has such an evil look, even by day, that the folk hereabouts shun it, for all the fine fish in it' (p. 58). Ann herself at this point openly expresses her fear of deep water: 'For my part, I cannot see deep water, running or still, without a shiver, like some harm will come to me from it' (pp. 58-9). Not long before her death she dreams of her father driving a flock of sheep into the sinister Llyn-tro. This parallels her earlier prophetic dream about her mother's death, but this time the dream foreshadows her own end. Through a series of small, apparently unconnected incidents the narrator builds up a sense of constant, lurking danger from beasts, elements and man. Ann's personal tragedy, the hopelessness of her attempts to avoid her inevitable fate, is set against the wider canvas of a nineteenth-century farming community where economic survival is a constant struggle, as unfavourable weather, flood, fire, and disease bring disaster to crops and stock. Nevertheless, the novel has its lighter moments which momentarily relieve the tension: the mischievous behaviour of the children, Ann hiding behind the settle to avoid the visiting parson, the sly, understated humour at the greed of Mrs Somers or the penny-pinching ways of Gwen Powys:

> Gwen Powys comes over to talk a bit, bringing some stockings to knit. She uses such hard coarse wool that we are all very sorry for her poor brother, it must be like walking in canvas.
> "I buy my wool for wear and not for show. Who sees Trefor's feet? And I knit very tight to make the wool go a long way."
> One day she will take to knitting his stockings out of binding twine, for I see her looking very hard at a ball of it on the table.
> (*Country Dance*, 73)

Brief as they are, these vignettes bring even the most minor characters vividly to life. But even such lighter incidents have ironic links with Ann's fate. She laughs at Gwen Powys's reading of her doom in the teacups and her talk of death-omens, but in the end the superstitious Gwen seems to be proved right. The narrative is short but full, and each incident, each conversation is directly connected with the progress of Ann's tale and the theme of the Border and its tensions.

Country Dance is technically extraordinarily polished and assured, especially for a first novel. But it is also remarkable for its strong female voice. Margiad Evans may not have regarded herself as a feminist, but it is not surprising that feminist critics in Wales are increasingly attracted to her work, especially to *Country Dance* (at present also the most easily available of her novels). In the introductory section the narrator immediately defines the story, in very modern terms, as an act of recovery of women's lost history in a world where it is men who are individualized and remembered:

> Circumstances have dimmed the memory of this woman and ironically accentuated that of the rivals, Gabriel Ford and Evan ap Evans, shepherd and farmer, Englishman and Welshman. The glare which at her death picked them out with horrible distinctness has left her curiously nebulous and unreal, a mere motive of tragedy.
> (*Country Dance*, vii)

Beneath the dramatic events, there is 'the subtler underlying narrative that bound the days together, the record of a mind rather than of actions' (p. 95). In telling Ann's story from the inside and in her own words, Margiad Evans relieves her of the status of victim, of disempowered girl helpless before male violence, and reasserts the image of a strong, capable woman, despite the inevitability of her fate. And although Ann is silenced by her death, her voice remains, for the wound on her temple 'cried aloud for justice', and the words that she wrote in 1850, and which ultimately led to her death, are recovered years later by the novelist who gives new life to them. Her liminal position in the undecided land between girlhood and marriage or spinsterhood exposes her to danger, but in the conclusion the author suggests that Ann's fate is more the consequence of her mixed blood than of her sex, and stems from the 'two nations at war' within her mind: 'Here is represented the entire history of the Border, just as the living Ann must have represented it herself', telling of 'incessant warfare' (p. 95). But gender is not irrelevant, for it is significant that the step which leads directly to her murder is her decision to throw in her lot with her *mother's* people, the Welsh, by agreeing to marry Evan ap Evans. On a personal level too there is an internal sexual conflict as her feelings for Evan ap Evans change from active dislike for his bullying tactics to unwilling attraction to him and eventually to her agreement to marry him. By the device of Ann's diary, Margiad Evans presents the events from an entirely female viewpoint. The narrative unfolds through Ann's own record of what she sees, hears and thinks, reflecting a life lived in the domain of women. In her rural world, women and men have their own, largely separate spheres, except for the busy periods of hay-making and harvest when all hands are needed to win the race against the weather. Otherwise they have their own tasks. Shepherding is for men, and only when her father is incapacitated by drink is Ann allowed to treat the sheep for scab. For women the world centres on the kitchen, cow-shed and dairy, on domestic activities such as cleaning, cooking, childcare, knitting and sewing. Much of their working and social life is spent with other women, baking, washing, gathering whinberries or blackberries, or dressing the dead, and these tasks provide the very framework of social inter-action, with constant opportunities for exchange of information, both public and private. The novel also pays tribute to women's work in a pre-technological society, from the hard physical labour of washing clothes to the lighter tasks such as sewing or topping and tailing gooseberries. It is no accident that our first visual image of Ann is of a young woman sitting at her work:

> While I am sewing the new curtains for the kitchen I see the par-son come up the hill in the snow. My mother goes to let him in, and he sits himself down before the fire to thaw a bit and drink the cup of tea we give him. My lap is full of snips and ends, which drop all over the floor when I stand up'.
> (*Country Dance*, 3-4)

Such details are not simply a backcloth to the story, but form the very rhythm of life for Ann and the other women and thus are fully integrated into the narrative, and the nature of the work in hand often suggests the time of year or day. Everything that happens to Ann, every step in the narrative, occurs in the context of one of these tasks or duties; even a journey must have a practical purpose.

The choice of a particular style for Ann's words helps to locate her story in an external time and place, but also reinforces the fact that hers is a voice recounting from within a private, female domain, from inside her own mind and social context. This is achieved by an understated, economical style, avoiding over-ripe description, but above all by the use of the present tense throughout Ann's diary, for recounting sequential events as well as her own reflections:

> I find there is no yeast for Thursday's baking, so I leave my mother sitting before the fire with her knitting and the door locked, because my father will be late, and go to Salus to fetch some.
>
> It is very dark and windy in the narrow lanes; when I cross the bridge I can hear the water is very near the top of the arches, and a glimmering here and there down in the meadows shows me the floods are out. Salus is empty, and well it may be on such a wild night; I get my yeast and am glad to set my feet on the way home, but the wind is dead against me and every inch is a struggle: the rain is falling in torrents so that it almost blinds me. I hear Tom Hill's cart coming; I know it by its one light and the clicking of the mare's hoofs. The light flickers over me, and Tom pulls up, calling me by name.
>
> (*Country Dance*, 6-7)

This use of the present tense never sounds artificial; on the contrary, it gives an extraordinary vividness, immediacy and intimacy to her tale, to the extent that, as the author notes in the introduction, it may give the reader 'the uncomfortable feeling of listening at a keyhole'. The technique can be traced back to oral storytelling traditions, especially those of women, and Margiad Evans may have heard Mrs Lloyd Jones of Coch-y-bûg using it, as it is particularly common in Welsh. Although in recent decades it has become more familiar to English-language readers through its use by writers in English of non-British origin, notably those from the Caribbean, in 1930 it must have been unusual and strange. And although she uses it with such confidence, the fact that Margiad Evans felt the need to justify it in her introduction suggests that she was uncertain how her readers would react.

THE BIRTH OF MARGIAD EVANS

Although the characters and plot of *Country Dance* are strong and well-defined, they are not the only players, for the main protagonist of the novel is the Border itself, especially in its capacity to both divide and unite. This is made explicit in the passage describing the supper at Tan-y-bryn, the home of Gwen Powys:

> Gwen has put out her blackberry wine; it sets the men to singing reckless words from 'Men of Harlech' despite [Gabriel's] mutters and angry looks.
> One of them jumps up from his place shouting:
> 'I drink to Wales!'
> Gabriel roars:
> 'And I to England!' and stands facing the other across the table. Megan and Margiad clap their hands; Mary looks serious.
> 'There'll be trouble in a minute, the men are hot as coals,' she whispers.
> Gwen purses her lips.
> 'I give the Border,' she says, very quiet.
> We all drink it down, and for once Mary and I have to forgo our laugh.
> (*Country Dance*, 60-1)

The message is reiterated in the epilogue, where it is explicitly linked with the nature of story in the popular memory in the Border country, a theme to which she would return in the 1940s in *Poems from Obscurity* and *The Old and the Young*:

> All old stories, even the authenticated, even the best remembered, are painted in greys and lavenders – dim, faint hues of the past which do no more than whisper of the glory of colour they once possessed. Yet live awhile in these remote places where these pale pictures were painted, and something of their first freshness will return to them, if only in the passing of a homestead or the mowing of a field. You will come to know how the dead may hold tenure of lands that were once theirs, and how echoes of their lives that are lost at a distance linger about their doorways. Here among the hills and valleys, the tall trees and swift rivers, the bland pastures and sullen woods, lie long shadows of things that have been.
> (*Country Dance*, 96)

Already in this short, early novel, Margiad Evans had forged her identity as a Border writer and published her manifesto.

Three
Haworth in Bridstow? (1933-1934)

Margiad Evans, as she had now become, had brought back from her stay in Pontllyfni more than just the manuscript draft of *Country Dance*. It was almost certainly this visit which had helped her choose the name she would henceforth use as a writer. The combination of that name and the subject-matter of *Country Dance*, together with its use of Welsh phrases and verses, led some readers and critics from both sides of the Border to assume she was Welsh, even Welsh-speaking. It was not her intention to take on a false Welsh identity: she would deceive neither herself nor others and took pains to correct any misapprehension on the matter. Although she was 'glad of my drop of Welsh blood', as she stressed years later in a letter to the Welsh writer and scholar Gwyn Jones in January 1946, she had never attempted to pose as Welsh. She stated this even more clearly to him a few weeks later: 'I'm *not* Welsh: I never posed as Welsh and it rather annoys me when R[obert] H[erring] advertises me among the Welsh short stories because *I am the border* – a very different thing. The English side of the border too. I don't speak fretfully: you know how I honour the Welsh writers'. These words were just as pertinent in 1930 when *Country Dance* appeared, and the Border, with its strange mixture of Welsh and English people and place-names and its resulting tensions and compromises, would continue to inspire and inform her writing throughout her life.

Not only did she stick to the name Margiad Evans, even if it misled people, but she also drew in her sister Nancy, who now became Sian Evans and made some attempts to emulate her older sister as a writer. In this she was not unsuccessful, for one of her short stories appeared in *The Welsh Review* in 1939 and another was included in anthologies. For all her encouragement of Nancy, comments in Margiad's journal in March 1933 show that she was sometimes afraid that her sister might outshine her as a writer. But she need not have worried, for although Nancy did not lack talent, she did not possess Margiad's motivation and determination in this field. In the notes on contributors in Gwyn Jones's Penguin collection of *Welsh Short Stories* (1940) Sian Evans characteristically states that she had 'always lived in the country and tried to be lazy, but necessity has often driven me to work'. The writer Arthur Calder Marshall, when visiting the Whistlers at Bridstow in May 1934, gained the distinct impression that Peggy was trying to create a trio of Evans sisters in Herefordshire to emulate the three Brontë sisters in Yorkshire, with Margiad casting herself as Emily and Sian 'rather reluctantly' playing Charlotte. 'Anne', he noted, 'was unfortunately not playing ball'. This was Betty, the eldest sister, whom he remembered as a very down-to-earth, no-nonsense woman.

That Margiad was deeply interested in Emily Brontë and indeed influenced by her is undeniable, and it seems likely that she was an important role model for the young woman novelist. It was not an unreasonable choice for a girl who was drawn to write and had grown up with two sisters and a younger brother in a rural environment. Emily Brontë was perhaps a more appropriate model than many of the other novelists whom Margiad Evans would have read by the time she was in her early twenties. Later on, her reading widened, but she never lost interest in Emily and it is a great pity that illness put paid to her planned full-length study of the writer she so admired.

Once Margiad Evans had completed *Country Dance*, and had it accepted for publication by Arthur Barker, she soon began to think of her next novel. It was not Barker, however, but Basil Blackwell who offered her an advance, so that she was able to concentrate on her writing for a time. This second novel, *The Wooden Doctor*, again draws on her stay at Pontllyfni, but in a very different way from *Country Dance*. It is also an utterly different novel. While *Country Dance*, although inspired by specific geographic locations, is largely a work of imagination, in terms of characters and plot *The Wooden*

Doctor is not drawn from her imagination but directly from her own life. The novel based on autobiography, closely related as it is to the journal form, has been a genre particularly favoured by women, especially for a first novel. Jeanette Winterson's *Oranges are not the only fruit* (1985), provides an obvious modern example, and in the nineteenth century the work of Charlotte Brontë, who may in fact have influenced Margiad Evans, as we shall see.

The autobiographical form has natural advantages for the woman writer working under restrictive circumstances. Being based on her own experience it requires no research away from home, but, more positively, it gives authority to her own voice and validates her experiences as an individual and as a woman. Like *Country Dance*, *The Wooden Doctor* takes the then radical step of presenting an uncompromisingly female view of the world as the norm, the standard against which the other sex is measured. Having successfully given voice to an imagined woman's experience in *Country Dance*, Margiad Evans in *The Wooden Doctor* now turns confidently to a telling of her own life. There may be an element of self-justification in this, as witness the fictional Arabella's comment that the doctor 'shall be seen by my light' (p. 153). Like Ann Goodman's diary, the narrative ensures that the woman's side of the story is heard and understood. But perhaps more importantly it also represents an attempt to make sense of events and feelings Margiad Evans had experienced, by submitting them to a process of selection, ordering and imaginative reworking, imposing a narrative structure on what had seemed without shape or order. The surviving draft of the novel represents an interim stage, for it includes much material which is undoubtedly drawn from her own life but has no obvious relevance to the central theme. The final version, reached after extensive revision, is pared down and more crisply focused.

The precise relationship between reality, as the young Peggy Whistler perceived it, and the imaginative retelling by Margiad Evans, is not easy to establish. In later life, notably in correspondence with Derek Savage, Margiad Evans was anxious to minimize the autobiographical nature of her fiction, and indeed the difference between the surviving draft of *The Wooden Doctor* and the published version shows how extensive was the editing process. Nonetheless, in its broad outlines much of the narrative of this novel conforms closely to known facts of her life or was confirmed later by the recollections of those who knew her, such as the Lloyd Jones family of Pontllyfni, or her former employers the Gadbans, who seem to be the model for the de Kuyper family in the novel. In the manuscript of the novel, moreover, she sometimes first wrote 'Peggy' instead of the fictional name 'Arabella', as if she had momentarily forgotten that she was ostensibly writing a novel, and had to correct herself. Similarly in the account of her stay in Caernarfonshire she originally kept the real names of people and places, and even in the published version she once refers to the fictional Gwynneth at Bodgynan as Minnie, the elder daughter at Coch-y-bûg. Margiad Evans did not always distance herself as novelist or narrator from herself as source, despite the rather disingenuous disclaimer at the beginning of this novel that 'all characters in this book are purely imaginary'. The reader should not be tempted, however, into believing that *The Wooden Doctor* is a 'true' account of her life, correct in all its details: it is not.

It opens, however, with a brief evocation of the year the two sisters spent with their aunt at Benhall, followed by the move to what is evidently Lavender Cottage with its wistaria whose 'twisted branches planted themselves around the veranda pillars' (p. xi). The close relationship between Arabella and her mother, becoming more difficult with the onset of adolescence, seems to reflect the author's own experience. So too does the fact that the mother is the more active parent, because the father, like John Goodman in *Country Dance*, has retreated into alcoholism. The first major section of *The Wooden Doctor* appears to be closely modelled on the writer's unhappy stay at the school in Loches, but has been subjected both to imaginative remodelling and literary influences. On the dust-jacket of *The Wooden Doctor* the publisher suggested 'an unconscious affinity with the author of *Villette*', and it is true that both Margiad Evans's Arabella and Charlotte Brontë's Lucy Snowe find themselves teaching abroad, alone and friendless in a francophone country, but befriended for a time by an Englishman, whose friendship is misconstrued. Minor characters at the Cours Saint-Louis, such as the pretty and flirtatious doorkeeper and the older professor of literature, also have their counterparts in *Villette*. Nevertheless, there are also closer parallels with *Jane Eyre*, notably in the restrictions and narrow religiosity of the regime, the cold of the building, and the inadequate food. In this respect the Cours Saint-Louis owes not a little to Lowood.

The rest of the narrative, recounting Arabella's stays in hospital, her visits to Oxfordshire and finally to Caernarfonshire, certainly derives from Margiad Evans's own experience, as does the account of Arabella's emergence first as an illustrator and then as a writer. Like the author, Arabella at twenty-one is commissioned 'to illustrate a collection of fables' and while staying with her cousin sets aside her artist's tools, picks up her fountain-pen and 'unscrewing it, travelled at once to green places where I had grown' (p. 152). What follows can only be a fictionalised account of the writing of *Country Dance*, culminating in its completion at Bodgynan/Coch-y-bûg. Even the author's amazed reaction to the publisher's letter accepting the book is recorded:

> ... out of the door I reeled in the sunshine, the same path where two months previously I had read my last letter from the Wooden Doctor. A wild dream, a fantasy had come true.
> I had never seriously considered anybody else looking upon my manuscript as more than a rather childish failure; I had found in it a refuge from thought, a cure for nostalgia.
> (*The Wooden Doctor*, 160)

Those last words, 'a refuge from thought, a cure for nostalgia', foreshadow her description of memories of childhood as 'a refuge for joy'. Already she had discovered the therapeutic value of selective, creative use of memories of the past, reordering and rewriting her own life.

The main theme of Margiad Evans's second novel is the love, or infatuation, of a young girl for a middle-aged doctor, an Irishman called Dr Flaherty, the 'wooden doctor' of the title. He was inspired by Dr John Leeper Dunlop (1883-1960), an Ulsterman who became the Whistler family's doctor in Ross. The feelings of the fictional Arabella undoubtedly mirror those of the author. Margiad herself analyses them in a letter to her husband in January 1946, whilst her cousin Kitty confirmed in 1963 that Margiad had been 'deeply in love' with Dr Dunlop and that it had taken her a long time to come to terms with his marriage. The doctor's widow told a similar story, recalling how for some time after their marriage Margiad telephoned and wrote constantly, despite her husband's attempts to discourage her. In the novel, when Arabella first meets him she is a twelve-year-old schoolgirl and he is 'about forty'. The narrative traces her increasing attraction to him despite the difference in age, an attachment which he does nothing to encourage, remaining 'wooden' although he treats her with unfailing kindness. In her later teens, however, Arabella's feelings intensify, parallelled by her increasing sufferings from agonizing bouts of cystitis, a particularly female complaint. In what must be the first literary description in English of cystitis attacks, Margiad Evans adopts the image of a fox tearing at her inside:

> In the night the pain came back. It was like a fox in a bag scratching and rending to get out. My spirits trailed in the dust. The claws penetrated my sleep, dragged me awake ...
> ... I learned how to keep off the dreadful fox by lying very still on my back: as soon as I sat up, the creature worried me relentlessly.
> (*The Wooden Doctor*, 77-8)

> Suddenly out of the darkness the fox sprang with flaming feet and famished jaws, rending, biting, tearing. I wished that I could faint and be delivered from this agony, but my strength increased with the torture.
> (p. 79-80)

Arabella's cystitis, unwoken during the first part of the novel, asserts itself when she returns home from a term at the Cours Saint-Louis in Touraine. Having encountered a young Englishman in France and had a mild flirtation with him, she is the more aware of her feelings for the unattainable doctor. It is his image that dominates the rest of the book as she is gradually but reluctantly forced to accept that he will never return her love and that she will never marry him. The progress of her love for him is intertwined with that of her physical illness, for it is her illness alone which enables Arabella, on the narrative level, to call the doctor to her; figuratively the pain of her sick body represents the suffering of her spirit. In that suffering and weakness lies her only power to bring the beloved doctor to her; only as his patient can she see him alone, and she believes that he alone can cure her because she loves him. Her faith in him is apparently confirmed by the failure of a hospital specialist to alleviate her physical disorder. As the novel's earlier title, 'The Divine Image' suggests, as well as idolizing the Irish doctor as a man, she has an almost religious belief in his healing powers. But the recurring image of the fox, the suffering and fever relieved only by the Irish doctor, and even the pain she feels as he examines her, become overt sexual metaphors, metaphors of her struggle with her developing sexual nature, a theme to which Margiad Evans would return in her next novel, *Turf or Stone*.

At the conclusion of *The Wooden Doctor*, Arabella seems for a time to have grown out of both doctor and cystitis, for during her stay in Caernarfonshire she has an affair with a young Englishman called Oliver and agrees to marry him. Once they are apart, however, she again falls prey to the fox, returns home the next day and by chance meets the doctor in the street. Immediately 'the conviction that I could not marry any other man' comes upon her. The return of her illness foreshadows her realization that the doctor means more to her than Oliver, perhaps an understanding that her love for Oliver was based chiefly on physical attraction. But she knows that the doctor will not see her as a woman: 'I could not attract the man I loved ... Twenty lovers would not atone for it' (pp. 145-6). For him she can only ever be 'a very brave child', and 'as a child he had treated me, my Papa-doctor, a tender and indulgent father' (p. 134), precisely the kind of father Arabella lacks but craves. The Freudian implications are obvious, but is unlikely that the author knew of Freud's work at this time.

Arabella's attempts to understand her developing sexuality are documented not only in her own relationships, with Julian at Loches and Oliver at Bodgynan, but also in her perceptions of other couples. The earliest example is her questioning of her mother's feelings for Arabella's father (p. xviii); later the relationship between Mademoiselle Dessier, headmistress of the Cours Saint-Louis, and her partner, Mademoiselle Baschet, parallels this in so far as the latter, like

Arabella's father, is the financial provider, but not the manager of the establishment. Later Arabella ponders the relationships of Mrs de Kuyper, sexually attractive and loved by two men, her husband and her secretary; she seems also to envy her cousin 'so contentedly blooming beside the husband she adored' (p. 145), her close and loving relationship with her husband and children representing an impossible ideal of marriage and maternity. Finally she notes how the retiring Mr Lloyd Owen at Bodgynan is bullied by his enormous wife: as with Arabella's own parents from the beginning of the novel, the husband is the minor character, an embarrassment to be kept in the background. None of these cases can provide a suitable model for Arabella, hence her inability to forget her idealized love for the doctor.

Her love makes her egotistical, for like a child she can only define him and others in relation to herself. This in turn gives her a sense of isolation from normal relationships, inevitable, she feels, for those in her situation:

> ... a charmed circle has been drawn around us. From the centre we see people and circumstances withdrawn at a distance into the shadows. There is no counting or reckoning. There is no communication.
> We are alone.
> (*The Wooden Doctor*, 130)

> Contented with my sole friendship, secure in its protection, I had looked out on other folk indifferently, or had expended the easy compassion with which one is born; now bereft of my own happiness, I fiercely resented the feast spread all around me which I could not share.
> (p. 156)

When she meets Oliver at the farm in north Wales Arabella is attracted to him partly because he offers a different model. He is not much older than her and has a character as strong and passionate as her own. But in the end her honesty enables her to see that marriage with him is not possible, for she is still not free from the 'divine image' she has created for the Irishman.

In terms of narrative structure *The Wooden Doctor* could scarcely be more different from Margiad Evans's first novel. The very formal, controlled structure of *Country Dance* gives way to a far looser, freer narrative, though handled with the same confidence. Whereas in *Country Dance* Ann's diary, flanked by two authorial passages, moves inevitably from the seeds of disaster to the fulfilment of disaster itself, the progress of *The Wooden Doctor*, because it is based on the author's own life, is far more leisurely and events are not always motivated by cause and effect. Furthermore, whilst there is scarcely a superfluous word in *Country Dance*, in *The Wooden Doctor* she allows herself longer passages of description and the luxury of loose ends, or ends only partly darned into the main fabric of the narrative.

There is still a first person narrator, Arabella, whose character, circumstances and experiences are founded on those of the author herself, and it is her voice which gives the narrative an element of unity. But the events are no longer circumscribed by a restricted time and place. In *Country Dance* everything happens within the compass of a few miles either side of the Border, but in *The Wooden Doctor* the action moves from Herefordshire to France, Oxfordshire and north-west Wales. Ann Goodman's diary documents less than a year of her life, but Arabella's narrative covers a period of many years, following her from puberty through adolescence until she becomes a woman, and it is this record of an individual growing up which gives the book such thematic and narrative structure as it possesses. It is almost as if, having proved in *Country Dance* that she could handle a narrative with complete control, Margiad Evans now felt that she could afford to experiment with the very opposite structure. Episode follows episode apparently as arbitrarily as in real life, with stops and starts, shifts of focus, and even self-conscious authorial intervention, long before that became a fashionable device. Although used sparingly, it enables her to remind the reader that a conventional romantic narrative is not her intention:

> 'This Arabella,' exclaims the befogged reader, 'how she does indulge herself in mental meanderings! I want a story, I want a hero, not a middle-aged doctor ... I want a pure, pretty and pursued heroine.' Good person, I am writing a history of humiliation and loss. It is for me: it is mine.
> (*The Wooden Doctor*, 160).

If the autobiographical framework of *The Wooden Doctor* partly accounts for its loose structure, it is also possible that the autobiographical form appealed to her precisely because it allowed her this greater freedom. It seems most likely that she wrote her second novel this way from choice, feeling no obligation to keep to any set of literary conventions imposed or expected by other people. This is also suggested by the authorial interventions in her later work, especially her fourth novel, *Creed* (1936).

The Wooden Doctor is a brave book, for in it Margiad Evans examines with unsparing honesty her failure to make her idealized and unresponsive beloved return her love, exposing her unrealistic expectations, self-deceit and eventual humiliation. She makes no attempt to soften or make more conventionally attractive the spiky character of her fictional representative Arabella, nor hide the egotism which makes it hard for her to admit failure but also allows her to cast off both Julian and Oliver with little thought for their feelings. In its consistent exclusion of the masculine viewpoint and its faithful recording of Arabella's adolescence and developing sexuality, it is also a very female book. This is made clear on the first page in a vivid but characteristically understated description of the elder sister's experience of puberty, a description not lacking in humour:

> Our elder sister [Catherine] went to boarding school; she appeared in the holidays, very tall and wearing beads. Her short crop had been allowed to grow into soft curls on her neck and her breast was no longer flat. We asked her if she did not find this uncomfortable? She said not in the least. She refused to bathe with us.
> (*The Wooden Doctor*, ix)

Arabella soon finds herself beginning to undergo similar changes:

> As we were undressing [Esther, her younger sister] told me that I should soon be like Catherine. I looked down at myself angrily, noticing faint curves of flesh.
> A servant had warned me that I would soon experience other changes. I awaited with fearful curiosity.
> (p. xii)

Arabella's fear and anger at the onset of puberty at the beginning of the novel suggest a wish to remain a child for longer, which is consistent with her later unwillingness to give up her love for the doctor. She does not want to 'grow out' of this immature love, but this means accepting that she can only be a child to him and that he can be no more than a father figure, her 'Papa-doctor'. But until she moves beyond this state she cannot have a more mature relationship with a man. Her first sexual encounter is no more than a step on the way to maturity, for she soon reverts to her old feelings for the Irishman; she has matured sexually but not emotionally. Oliver may have 'stirred [her] blood' but she has gained no real knowledge or understanding of him. She still sees men through the egotistical eyes of a child and still inhabits a largely female domain, lacking the means of proper communication with men as individuals. Her home life was dominated by mother and sister, men are the exception at the Cours Saint-Louis, and her stay in Oxfordshire centres on her cousin and her two daughters, the novelist husband appearing as a peripheral character. Above all, the hospital where she undergoes tests is a women's world of patients, nurses and matron, where men rarely intrude and never without female escort. Her stays there define Arabella as one belonging to the enclosed world of female illness, where pain crosses boundaries of age and condition which would otherwise separate the women. It gives her a glimpse of an adult world, but one where in the communality of a large ward individuals can still be isolated from each other by fear and suffering, and the women patients are infantilized, told off as 'naughty girls' if pain makes them cry out. At the end of the novel Arabella has progressed from her pre-pubertal state at the beginning but the journey is not complete. The next stage would be explored in *Turf or Stone*.

The Wooden Doctor was published by Blackwell on 16 March 1933, the day before her twenty-fourth birthday. She refers to it in her journal as her first novel, perhaps because she considered *Country Dance* more of a long short story. She had sent a proof copy to Dr Dunlop, the Irish doctor who had inspired the book, but she had no response, perhaps because he was ill at the time. She had designed the novel's dust-jacket and its striking black and white frontispiece, both signed 'PW': she was still using the name Peggy Whistler for her visual work. The result pleased her. 'It's a pretty book, nicely bound', she wrote in her journal, noting with satisfaction when the *Daily Mail* reproduced the frontispiece with a review of the book that 'nobody knows I did that too'. The reviews were generally favourable. Compton Mackenzie, the *Daily Mail* reviewer, described it as 'really good' and the other national newspapers echoed his praise. 'Heavens! ... this young woman can write' enthused James Agate in the *Daily Express*, with perhaps a slightly patronising undertone. By the time *Creed* was published in 1936 *The Wooden Doctor* was already into its third impression. Margiad Evans later used to say of her work as a whole that it had had no financial success, but she may have meant that she had never earned enough to live on comfortably; since Basil Blackwell was prepared to offer her an advance on what would be her third novel, he cannot have been dissatisfied with the sales so far. Whether he appreciated her warm affection for him is not known. However, he must have been aware that this young woman, who could not look up to her own father, had already fixed on one father-figure, the Irish doctor, and with that episode now closed was beginning to view Basil Blackwell in a similar light as a kind of surrogate father. For her he was 'the Professor', another sign of the influence of Charlotte Brontë, and he began to call her Arabella after her *alter ego* in *The Wooden Doctor*. In her journals, where she also refers to herself at this time as Arabella, she even fantasized about what it would be like to be married to him.

At this period Margiad was living about twenty-five miles from Oxford in the Cotswold village of Asthall, between Burford and Witney. Asthall was the next village to Swinbrook, the home of her cousin Dorothea Churchill-Longman, through whom she probably found and rented Asthall School Cottage, where she was joined by her sister Nancy. The Whistler sisters seem to have lived at Asthall for about a year, Peggy trying to make progress with her next novel but also leading a busy social life. In February 1933, however, when Basil Blackwell with his wife and children came to visit, she was able to show him the opening section of her new book, *Turf or Stone*, and to her great relief, he liked it. He believed in her work, he told her, and would do all he could to ensure its success. By this time she was disillusioned with Arthur Barker, who had published *Country*

Dance. She felt that he had made less effort to push her work than Blackwell seemed prepared to do, but there was also another reason: he was trying to get her into bed with him. She did not want to mix business and private life and in any case he did not attract her. 'Artie', she complained in her journal on 27 February, '... would have our relationship too personal, but sorry though I am for him I won't sleep with him. That makes him vinegary sometimes. He isn't very interested in my work so I shall try to break away from him and stay with Basil Blackwell'. Five weeks later, on 6 April 1933, Margiad went to Oxford to meet Barker and he agreed to let her go. That evening she saw Blackwell at his office and 'he is now my publisher for good and always.'

On 1 March 1933 the Whistler sisters received notice to quit School Cottage. In her journal Margiad put this down to their entertaining a young man called Percy Oliver until four o'clock one morning. They returned home to Bridstow and the summer was spent mainly at Lavender Cottage. Judging by her journal she was making very slow progress with *Turf or Stone*. Although the main character, Easter Probert, was already formed in her mind and she tried to write regularly, she seemed to advance very little. 'After creating a world for myself where I'm God and making people, it should be easy enough to manoeuvre them. But it's not easy', she noted that August. 'Often I write only a few words a day and that's hateful to me.' Things were no better at the beginning of September: 'Everything seems to elude me before I can pin it on paper, like eels'. It was a hot summer and she found herself easily distracted from her writing. When visitors stayed at the house Margiad and Nancy had to share a bedroom, and at other times too Nancy tended to wander in and out so she had none of the peace and solitude she craved. In mid August she went to visit a friend in Oxford but suffered an attack of her old trouble, cystitis. She was run down, perhaps anaemic, and low in spirits. The situation was not improved by tensions between Margiad and her parents, especially her mother. Until well into her teens, she wrote later in 'The Immortal Hospital', she had loved her mother so dearly that she could 'never leave her without tears', but during the periods she spent at home in her early twenties Margiad was often infuriated by her. Her father, on the other hand, emerges from the journal as a rather bemused, eccentric creature, often drunk, exasperating but pitiable. He appeared mainly at meal-times, or would be heard staggering in after an evening at the pub.

Despite all the distractions which made work on the novel such a struggle, she did manage to produce at least two short stories, which she sent to Basil Blackwell. He liked them, and she was pleased that he thought one of them, entitled 'Mrs Parry', 'the most charming thing you've written'. It is a delicate tale of an old lady living alone in an almshouse in increasing poverty and ill health. When she is taken into the workhouse infirmary for the winter the two sisters who visit her, obviously Margiad and Sian, fear she will never come out, but spring finds Mrs Parry back home, herself and the cottage spruced up. Margiad Evans's journal shows that this was a true story thinly disguised.

By October 1933 she had to admit that *Turf or Stone* would never be finished in the atmosphere of Lavender Cottage. With Blackwell pressing her to complete the novel Margiad had to find somewhere else to write. She took herself off to stay at the Lough Pool Inn at Sellack, about three miles north-west of Bridstow. It was just far enough away, in the days before cars were common, to ensure she was not constantly disturbed, but near enough for her to see Nancy and their friend Marjorie Byolin, who also lived in Bridstow. Even today the inn is a secluded, out-of-the-way place, not easy for strangers to find. Opposite the half-timbered inn lies the pool from which it takes its name, or rather it sometimes does, for it only fills with water after heavy rain. Day after day Margiad sat writing at the table in her upstairs room, a little box lined with a rose-printed wallpaper, but with a window each side, one looking out towards the road, the other onto the orchard behind the inn. After a slow start her confidence returned. She started by writing a couple of short stories as a warm-up exercise. One she destroyed, having found that Nancy had written 'almost the same thing', but she was better pleased with the other, entitled 'The Wicked Woman', later to be included in her collection, *The Old and the Young*. The setting is probably the Lough Pool Inn, and she noted in her journal that the narrative was based on 'things I heard'. She immediately sent 'The

Wicked Woman' to Hamish Miles, who accepted it for publication in *Life and Letters*.

Three days into her stay, on 17 October, she was well into the novel. By 20 October she calculated that she was over half way through the novel: 'I shall do it'. By the time she emerged, exhausted, on 3 December after her seven weeks' retreat, she had not only finished the draft of *Turf or Stone* but had three more stories to send to Hamish Miles. Back at Lavender Cottage she began revising the novel, a process she hated. However, she must have met Blackwell's deadline of 14 January 1934 for submission of the final draft, because by mid February the first proofs had arrived.

A pattern had established itself by now. She would have a period of comparative idleness as the next novel gestated, though usually with the discipline of keeping her journal. This was then followed by a period of intense activity. The drafting of the novel would be undertaken in a remarkably short period, often writing late into the night, fortified with coffee and especially cigarettes. Throughout her life she smoked heavily and was rarely seen without a 'Craven A' in her mouth.

In *Turf or Stone* she returned to depicting a rural community, as she had done in *Country Dance*, but now the action is restricted to the English side of the Border, in the countryside around Ross that Margiad Evans knew so well. Wales is always present in the background, however, in the Welsh surnames and in the origins of some of the characters. Dorothy Kilminster, despite her very English manner, is from Cardiff, and her widowed mother, Eirian Thomas, once known as 'the Welsh Nightingale', still sings Welsh songs; Harry Lloyd, landlord of 'The Dog', is from Glamorgan and so has difficulty understanding the mentality of his wife, who comes from a Caernarfonshire village. The novel is set in the present, in the late 1920s or early 1930s. The First World War is long over, but the granite war memorial and the one-armed carter provide quiet reminders of its effect on the community. Money is short amongst the drinkers in the pub but middle-class women drink coffee, and smoke cigarettes in public. Horses are still essential forms of transport, but cars drive past in increasing numbers. District nurses and county schools have arrived. Political change is in the air too, and social distinctions are becoming less rigid. Middle-class families still must have servants, but Matt Kilminster, gentleman farmer and *rentier*, with a 'fairly large income from Welsh breweries' has a 'strong leaning towards democracy' and 'associated with whom he liked', especially when it came to drinking companions. Mary Bicknor, a proud and affected 'half servant, half companion to an eccentric old lady', whose social standing is defined by her expensive silk underwear, finds herself pregnant by Matt Kilminster's groom, the rough, boorish Easter Probert, a development of the character of Evan ap Evans in *Country Dance*. She is forced to marry this man below her presumed station, but later becomes mistress to Kilminster himself.

In this time of uncertainty accepted social values are being rapidly undermined. The family and marriage provide neither comfort nor stability and are portrayed as empty, meaningless institutions. Not one single marriage in the novel is a happy or satisfactory one. Easter refuses to allow his forced marriage to the pregnant Mary to change his womanizing, bullying ways, and much of the novel is concerned with Mary's attempts to escape from him. Matt and Dorothy Kilminster are failures both as marriage partners and parents, they are bored with each other, there is no real communication between them and they take little responsibility for either themselves or their children. Ironically, Matt's adulterous relationship with Mary seems more sincerely loving than that with his wife, and those characters showing the greatest warmth and concern for others, Phoebe's grandmother and the carter, are both widowed. Legal institutions are discredited: just as the marriage ceremony performed by the vicar at the beginning of the novel cannot make a true marriage between Easter and Mary, neither can legal processes rescue Mary from her husband's cruelty. In the court case at the end of the novel it is Mary, not the defendant Easter, who suffers most, and this very modern perception of the treatment of women in cases of sexual violence must have seemed very radical at the time. In the end it is not the law which releases her from her husband but the jealous Tom Queary, taking the law into his own hands by murdering Easter with a pike.

In *Turf or Stone* Margiad Evans no longer presents her narrative through a first person, female voice. Instead an omniscient narrator follows each of the main characters in turn, and for the first time in her published work she brings male characters to the forefront. The two central figures are Matt Kilminster and his groom, the gipsyish Easter Probert, and the action focuses on the intertwining of their lives, from Easter's forced marriage with Mary Bicknor to his trial for cruelty to her, followed swiftly by his violent death. Easter's ill-matched union with Mary is parallelled by Matt's virtually dead marriage to Dorothy, who is interested only in her appearance, trivial pastimes, and her little son, whom she treats more as a doll or a pet than as a developing individual. The two men's roles are complementary. At first Matt is the serious drinker and Easter the womaniser but in the course of the novel their roles are reversed, with Easter drinking more heavily and finally lacking a partner after years of promiscuity, and Matt taking a mistress for the first time.

In the middle, between the two couples, stands Phoebe, the Kilminsters' eldest daughter, who is fifteen years old when the story begins. Phoebe is distanced from the rest of her family, even from her sister Rosamund, and only enjoys a close relationship with her Welsh grandmother. In the course of the novel, however, she becomes increasingly drawn to the rough and violent Easter Probert, even after she has discovered with disgust that her father is having an affair with Easter's wife. Although some events are seen through Phoebe's eyes, it is Easter himself who dominates the book, for Margiad Evans had found herself 'obsessed, almost possessed by [his] strange character' (journal, 9 April 1933). With the focus on a man, the settings are naturally very different from those in Margiad Evans's first two novels. In *Turf or Stone* much of the action takes place in the masculine domains of pubs, cattle-market, Easter's various filthy lodgings, or outdoors. The fact that Matt is a less conventionally masculine character than Easter is suggested not only by the fact that he does no work, but also by his spending so much time indoors. He may be the master but he has no strength or authority, and though he enjoys riding, he falls off his horse, a further sign of weakness. Since Easter is the main protagonist, it is natural that a number of episodes should be located in inns, but this may also be connected with the circumstances in which Margiad Evans wrote the novel at the Lough Pool Inn. Mr Preece, the landlord, told her stories, tap-room sounds reached her room, and she sometimes went down to the bar and observed the drinkers, listening to their talk.

Lacking the consistent focus of the first-person narrator, the narrative of *Turf or Stone* is more fragmented than the two earlier novels, even though it has more of a plot in the conventional sense. Having decided that the central character of Easter was to give the novel its cohesion, the author was aware of the problems that this posed in making the other characters 'sufficient[ly] strong to live' since they are only 'shadows to him' (journal, 9 April 1933). Perhaps this is why she decided to let the narrative unfold through the eyes of a number of characters, rather than Easter alone, but whilst this enables us to see Easter from a variety of perspectives it tends also to shift our attention from him too much at times. The problem of creating sufficiently rounded characters apart from Easter is aggravated by the fact that the novel contains too much material peripheral to the main thread of the narrative, material which is not satisfactorily integrated. Very minor characters are brought into the foreground, named and set in their social context, thus raising expectations of their importance, but they are then dropped, to be linked only rather adventitiously to the main narrative in what seems like an afterthought. Sometimes these marginal characters may have been suggested by their origins in Margiad Evans's own life. Jack Lewis, for example, the pig butcher who returns to invite Easter Probert to join him in a business venture, was suggested by the author's handsome cousin, whom she recalls in 'The Immortal Hospital' as Robbie. In that account he was a young man with romantic looks who had an escapade with her uncle's milk-float at Benhall and eventually married a barmaid and disappeared. In the novel, the timing and motivation of Jack's reappearance in search of Easter are unconvincing, as if he had walked in from another story. The author's own interest in her delinquent cousin seems to be the main reason for including this character, although she does use it as a rather artificial device to reveal that Matt has been effectively paying Easter for the use of his wife.

The author had not yet learned to integrate fully such material borrowed from life into the narrative as she later did in *The Old and the Young*, and in *Turf or Stone* a number of incidents or conversations seem to have been included more because they had caught the author's fancy than because they are essential to the action, for example, an anecdote about an old lady persuaded to keep a donkey to eat the thistles in her paddock. And in another echo of the autobiographical *The Wooden Doctor*, Phoebe Kilminster's grandmother, Eirian Thomas, married at twenty-four a doctor whom she had first met when she was twelve and he already a man. It is no surprise, then, to find that Phoebe, who has much of the young Peggy Whistler in her, is herself twelve years old when Easter Probert first comes to work as her father's groom, and the relationship between Phoebe and her younger sister, Rosamund, has more than a passing resemblance to that between Peggy and Nancy. Although the book is dedicated 'to my father who does not resemble Matt', his drinking and interest in otter-hunting inevitably recall Godfrey Whistler. It is almost as if Margiad Evans, having decided to write a novel with a stronger foundation in imagination, could still not resist the temptation to include these details drawn so obviously from her own life.

There were literary influences, too. In a letter to Derek Savage, dated 24 March 1950, she suggested that Easter Probert was 'a study of Byron in whom I am very much interested. It was at the time unconscious, but I still think it a true interpretation of Byron's personality'. She was probably referring to Easter's womanizing behaviour, forever searching for a substitute for the Mrs Fitzgerald whom he had loved as a boy:

> A gentle, timid woman he might have loved with real intensity, and perhaps even constancy, since his promiscuous rovings were something in the nature of a search.
> (*Turf or Stone*, 79)

> Mrs Fitzgerald had haunted his childhood with her nakedness, and she haunted his manhood also ... he lusted after women from this time onwards, but his lonely and abandoned spirit dwelt in a wilderness where as yet none had ever penetrated. None. Never.... He disliked men, and longed in the bottom of his heart for a woman's tenderness. But he had not the least idea how to arouse it, and invariably went wrong from the beginning.
> (p. 104)

Like Byron too, he makes an unsuitable marriage to a woman who considers herself superior to him, and having been consistently unfaithful to her, finds her suing for separation on grounds of cruelty. He is prevented from ever finding his ideal by the conflict between his wish for his lovers to be docile or to mother him tenderly and his desire to bully them. Some women, the stronger ones, use him only as he has used others, and drop him when they are ready to move on; only the seventeen-year-old Phoebe in the final section of the novel seems able to accept him as he is and offer a more honest, if immature, response. What she offers comes too late, however, for any consummation or even resolution of their relationship is prevented by Easter's violent death, just as in *Country Dance* Ann Goodman's union with Easter's forerunner, Evan ap Evans, is stopped by her murder. Reading *Turf or Stone* in the light of Margiad Evans's later essay on Byron and Emily Brontë, it could be argued that Easter Probert is killed just at the point when he has a chance to mature and leave behind his rather childish fury against a society which disgusted him.

If Byron was one model, albeit an unconscious one, for Easter Probert another was probably Emily Brontë's Heathcliff. Like Heathcliff, Easter is small and stocky, dark-skinned and dark-eyed, of uncertain ancestry but presumed to be of gipsy blood. Like Heathcliff, he deliberately flouts conventional notions of decent behaviour. He is calculating, but also driven by strong emotions, although these are not focused on one woman as they are in Emily Brontë's hero. But Easter shares with the latter a cruel and bullying nature, and an inability to sympathise with the feelings of others. Both of them are essentially egotistical, and it is this which gives them their power. But it is also their downfall. Whereas it is Heathcliff's obsessive love for Cathy which drives him and eventually leads to his death, it is Easter's proud unconcern for others which destroys him, since it is his loveless, selfish sexual relationship with Emily Queary which causes her husband to murder him. In a sense, Easter is a larger, masculine version of the Arabella of *The Wooden Doctor*, in so far as he, like her, is a wounded soul isolated by egotism from normal human communication. But whereas Arabella, like some female Heathcliff, is driven by a single obsessive love for one man, from whom other men can offer only a temporary distraction, Easter lacks a single object of love, in marriage or outside it. And whilst Arabella feels for the doctor a love which can never be physically consummated, Easter is driven by lust which is constantly gratified. It is only towards the end of the novel, when Phoebe seems to offer him a new choice, that 'for the first time he was moved a little beyond his predatory senses' (p. 273). For both Arabella and Easter, lust may be gratified but love will never be consummated.

Phoebe's role in *Turf or Stone* is a complex one, and is not fully worked out. Even Margiad Evans's obsession with Easter could not prevent her shifting her attention from time to time to this key female figure who has more than a little of herself in her situation and character. It is significant that, for all her obsession with Easter, it is a line-drawing of Phoebe that she provided for the dust-jacket, and that drawing is an obvious self-portrait. In a sense, Phoebe provides a counterpoint to Easter, the young, virginal girl of higher social class contrasting with the rough, promiscuous, older man who works for her father. It is Phoebe too who provides a further continuity with *The Wooden Doctor*, for here again the author explores the theme of a young girl trying to come to terms with her developing sexuality. Both Arabella and Phoebe are drawn towards older men, whom they first encountered when they were twelve years old and thus approaching menarche, but Phoebe is not driven by Arabella's consuming love and desire for marriage with the beloved. And whereas Arabella's first sexual encounter is with a conventional figure, a personable young man, Phoebe's first sexual feelings are kindled by the apparently highly unsuitable groom. In the final interview between Phoebe and Easter Margiad Evans subtly and delicately traces the development of a new understanding of each other, and the hope, later dashed by Easter's murder, of a more honest communication between them. There is a gradual shift in Phoebe's attitude to Easter in the course of the novel as she begins to see him not just as her father's servant but as a man, and comes to understand that it is possible for a woman to be sexually attracted to a man whom she does not love and whom she may at times hate, fear or despise.

Just as in *The Wooden Doctor* Arabella learns to differentiate sexual passion from an emotional state of love, in *Turf or Stone* women as well as men are able to separate sexual desire from love. Apart from Phoebe with her emergent sexual feelings towards Easter, there are a number of women characters in *Turf or Stone* whose relationships with men are driven solely by sexual attraction. After his marriage Easter Probert has a series of affairs with women, married and unmarried, none of whom show any symptoms of romantic love for him, and who are obviously using him just as he does them. It is striking that not all of these women passively wait for him to leave them. Some are strong enough to end the relationship themselves, for they are as capable as he is of sexual and emotional independence. Since so many of the relationships portrayed in this novel are selfish and loveless, the overall impression is dark and depressing, in keeping perhaps with the novelist's own mood during the book's gestation. American reviewers in particular found it excessively grim. There are chinks of light, however, in the rare hints that greater warmth and better communication can be possible between human beings, for example in the kindness of the widowed, warmaimed carter to the wretched Mary, or Phoebe's new understanding of Easter. In both cases Margiad Evans suggests some small hope for human relations, but in both cases, in Hardyesque fashion, this happier possibility is offered too late.

Turf or Stone is perhaps the least satisfactory of Margiad Evans's novels in terms of its construction and its perhaps excessively gloomy and cynical view of life. But in spite of a lack of cohesion on a narrative level, it has a firm internal consistency precisely because it echoes the author's strongly felt attitude to human relationships at the time of writing. Its unity of tone, barely disturbed by quieter, calmer interludes such as Phoebe's stay at her grandmother's home, reflects exactly the mood of the novelist's contemporary journal, full of bitterness and tension as she strives to understand and accept her self. If *The Wooden Doctor* was overtly autobiographical in the external events it recounted, *Turf or Stone*, for all its imaginative setting and plot, can be described as an internal autobiography, a mapping through fiction of the writer's own inner life, both emotional and intellectual.

Four
Translating What I Have Learned
(1934-1936)

Margiad Evans spent the first months of 1934 at Bridstow, nervously waiting for *Turf or Stone* to come out. Her journal reveals that she felt deeply unsettled and dissatisfied with herself, and these feelings break out periodically in a passionate fury of self-loathing and of hatred or contempt for others, especially her mother. Whether these black emotions were openly expressed is not clear, but it seems that her journal acted as a safety valve for letting off steam in private. 'I write all this because I want to forget it', she wrote in the autumn of 1939: 'I always write what I want to get rid of'. This is confirmed by the difference in tone between her journals and correspondence in the mid and late 1930s. Later, maybe a little ashamed of some of these dramatic and negative outpourings, she carefully blacked out in Indian ink some of the more disturbing paragraphs. Perhaps she had had to grow up too quickly, leaving school at sixteen and trying to survive alone, abroad, and as a result had not been able to give full rein to adolescent rebellion at the usual time. And having tasted the freedom of living independently, away from home, it must have been frustratingly hard to live within the family again. She wanted to define herself as a professional writer, but she was still dependent on her family, and she knew it. It was her father's 'tiny pension', as she told Derek Savage in 1950, which 'had insured [*sic*] me of a home where I could at least correct the rough drafts of my stories, always written on a small advance from the publisher'. Blackwell's advances were enough to motivate her to write the next book, but not enough to live on.

TRANSLATING WHAT I HAVE LEARNED

At home she made a new friend, Ruth Farr, who lived at Tretire Court about four miles west of Bridstow. Mrs Whistler brought her to stay at Lavender Cottage in February 1934 after Ruth had a row with her mother. Margiad did not at first take to Ruth, whom she described in her journal as 'a confessed and obvious Lesbian', but after a rather tense start they became deeply involved and remained friends for many years afterwards. At the time of Margiad's first meeting with Ruth the family was busy with preparations for the wedding of the eldest of the Whistler girls, Betty, who married a doctor, William Pratt, on 27 February in Bridstow church. Less than a month later, when Betty was settled into her new home in London, Margiad and Nancy went to stay with her. This seems to have been Margiad's first entry into London literary life. On 27 March they met Arthur Calder Marshall at a sherry party. He later recalled that he had first come across Margiad Evans's work when a friend brought *The Wooden Doctor* to his attention. Being then on the editorial board of *New Stories* which Basil Blackwell was publishing, he invited her to contribute but she had nothing suitable to send at the time. However, this first contact had led to a correspondence and they arranged to meet whilst Margiad was staying with Betty. To Margiad he did not seem a very attractive figure, but 'a shortish young man whose eyes are peculiar, slatey opaque'. Nancy got on with him better than Margiad did. He was very attentive, taking them to exhibitions and even inviting them to supper in his flat. They sat round a tiny table eating roast mutton and were introduced to the wife of the publisher Fredric Warburg, invited specially to meet the sisters. Margiad did not take to her and described her in her journal as 'a bitch of [a] hussy'. She was interested in making contacts in London but judged those she met by her own standards rather than by what they represented or how important they might be.

The sisters also visited Arthur Barker, with whom Margiad was still on friendly terms, and met for the first time the writer and critic David Garnett. Margiad took him a short story, 'The Red Umbrella', about the relationship between a woman, her husband and her brother, and he accepted it for the *New Statesman and Nation*, where it appeared in May that year. That this visit was very much a joint enterprise for Peggy/Margiad and Nancy/Sian as writers as well as sisters is evident from the fact that they went everywhere together and David Garnett was offered and took one of Sian's stories too. He was less taken with the 'lovely and pretty pineapple' the Whistler sisters presented to him. He carried it round for a while, dangling it from his hand by a hook, then conveniently lost it.

In spite of some negative comments in her journal, Margiad seems to have relished this stay in London and the chance to meet other writers. There were also family visits, notably a trip to Uxbridge to visit her aunt Nell, which brought back sudden, distinct memories of her earliest years before the family moved to Herefordshire. In the garden, unchanged after twenty years, she seemed to glimpse the little girl she once was, running with an egg in a spoon on the grass beside the river at the bottom of the garden. This led her to reflect, as she would later in her poetry and short stories, on the identity of the self through different ages. The child she remembered at Aunt Nell's 'was the same person, exactly the same being, as the freezing young woman with her shoulders wrapped in a rug, looking at the hyacinths... I might have been there yesterday, a child: I was there today as a woman'. Perhaps the river at Uxbridge also reminded her of her first, deeply formative sight of the Wye.

She returned to Bridstow refreshed by her jaunts but soon began to lapse into gloom, which was not dispelled by another visit to Wales in June. This time she went for a holiday at Southerndown on the Glamorganshire coast, but its seaside charms could not compete with Pontllyfni and the mountains of Snowdonia.

Her next novel, *Creed*, whose atmosphere reflects the black period she was still going through, was longer in the making than its predecessors, and there was a gap of two years between the publication of *Turf or Stone* and this new work, which she completed in January 1936. Life at home became even less easy during her father's last illness in the autumn and winter of 1935, and the mood was no better in the wider world, with unemployment and poverty in Britain and the rise of Hitler already beginning to threaten another European war. Nevertheless, even the darkest sections of her journal are suddenly lightened when she becomes absorbed in observation of the life of the countryside:

> ...along the hill top Maile is guiding a squeaking harrow: later on
> he brings the nebulous horses to the stable, clanking with har-
> ness and breathing steam into the light of my lamp, which clings
> to the harsh cast of his face.
> (27 November 1935)

By now Margiad was becoming increasingly established as writer,
and her visit to London in March 1934 had helped to consolidate her
position. In May that year, practically the same day as 'The Red
Umbrella' appeared in the *New Statesman*, Arthur Calder Marshall
came to stay with the Whistlers at Bridstow. Describing this visit to
Arnold Thorpe in 1963, Calder Marshall admitted that much of the
blame for its awkwardness lay on his side. According to his account,
nearly thirty years after the event, this was their first meeting, but
Margiad's journal proves that they had already met in London on
more than one occasion. In explaining why his visit to Lavender
Cottage was not a success, Calder Marshall pleaded that he was
only twenty-three at the time, with his intellect over-developed at
the expense of his emotional development. Worst of all, he had
taken into the romantic head that lay beneath his veneer of sophis-
tication, the idea that this young woman writer would be the girl of
his dreams. She was not. This later account of disillusionment at his
first meeting with Margiad makes a good story, but as he had in fact
seen her before, he must have already realized when they met in
London that she was not to be his ideal.

He found her interesting but not attractive, but was much struck
by her strong, pale face and black hair. He found the more pliant
Nancy more sympathetic, as Margiad had surmised when they first
met. Margiad herself was perhaps too strong a personality for him.
In her own contemporary account of his visit to Lavender Cottage,
Margiad notes that he wore 'dirty slack clothes, sat on the coal box
and wrote reviews when he could'. In London, where she was the
visitor, they had got on well, but now that he was temporarily trans-
planted to her world in Bridstow, she felt awkward and unsettled.
Whilst Nancy, more relaxed, took him tea in bed in the mornings
and sat on the bed talking to him, Margiad ran about 'like a pea-hen

in dingy black; my hair was tangled, my face a drift of powder'. In his account Calder Marshall, to support his contention that she was play-acting and identifying with the Brontë sisters, emphasizes that she wore a 'distinctively Victorian habit of black serge' in which she strode, Emily-like. This portrait contrasts sharply with the memories of Marjorie Byolin, a close friend of the Whistler sisters at Bridstow during these years, for she described the girls to Arnold Thorpe in 1965 as 'bohemian' rather than Victorian in appearance. Unusually for the mid 1930s, she recalled, they often wore trousers, as an 'act of defiance'. The eye of a female friend and neighbour differed from that of the male visitor from London. Margiad herself often refers in her journal to wearing trousers, not for the sake of a bohemian image, but more as an index of her general slovenliness. She describes herself in September 1933 as 'an unkempt, ungroomed object. My nails are often dirty, and always neglected ... my hair unglossy.' Only her complexion, she adds, received much attention.

Although Arthur Calder Marshall and Margiad Evans never became close friends, they remained in touch sporadically until the war, and briefly resumed their correspondence when *A Ray of Darkness* was published in 1952. If she did not take up his invitation to contribute to *New Stories* it was probably because she had already offered elsewhere any finished work. Among her manuscripts only one unpublished story from this period can be traced. This is a companion piece to the earlier 'Mrs Parry', for it describes the same two sisters visiting a local girl, ill with pneumonia in the workhouse infirmary. Again it is inspired by actual events, as Margiad's journal for June 1934 confirms. The tale of Lizzy Ford, like 'Mrs Parry', is a slight but fascinating forerunner of the stories she wrote in the 1940s.

Although Lizzy Ford, like Mrs Parry, is cured and returns home, the final section dwells more on the narrator's guilt at a broken promise than on the happiness of the girl's recovery. Like *Creed*, with its even darker atmosphere, this story reflects the author's mood at the time of writing. But the new novel also presents a continuum with her previous published work. Like *Turf or Stone* it has violent characters with a disregard for the accepted rules of social behaviour, and it again picks up the theme of female sexuality. But whereas in *Turf or Stone* Emily Brontë and Byron were unmistakable influences, in *Creed* the Bible was a powerful inspiration, as she told Derek Savage in April 1950: '*Creed* ... is the story of Job, that incredibly great masterpiece of prose and poetry with so weak a conclusion.'

Like the Book of Job, *Creed* explores the relationship between man and God. Judging by her journals, Margiad Evans was at this time preoccupied with the question of belief in God and attempting to formulate her own position. She asks herself whether true belief in God must be preceded by unbelief, an idea reflected in the novel, together with the paradox that truly knowing and loving God does not necessarily lead to peace and happiness. On the contrary, the godless may often apparently live more untroubled lives than do the godly, a theme which had been touched upon in *The Wooden Doctor* in a discussion between Arabella and a visiting preacher. *Creed* opens with an extraordinary sermon by the Reverend Ifor Morriss, parson of a rural parish a few miles away from the town of Chepsford, a disreputable man, known to drink, keep bad company and possibly steal money from the Church. Morriss, as his sermon reveals, is reacting against his Welsh father, a Nonconformist minister near Bala and 'a stony, rigid believer, an inexorable teacher who inflicted religion on me like a punishment'. Taking his text from the Book of Job, Ifor Morriss argues that God honoured Job's integrity, 'yet Job could sin'. God, therefore, loves the sinner, and God is always in man, even in the worst sinner, even a murderer:

> 'I believe that for us all there is no spiritual death or torment though we may have earned it. We are sinners, but our Redeemer liveth – He liveth *here*'. Ifor Morriss put his hand upon himself.
> (*Creed*, 8)

After the service Morriss is visited by Francis Dollbright, a clerk from Chepsford, whose own faith resembles that of the parson's father and whose harsh beliefs have made him inward-looking. He has become indifferent to the fate of his neighbours, in both the literal and the Christian sense of the term.

Those neighbours, in their various ways and for different reasons, also emerge as sufferers. In general, the working people of the town are depicted as a careless lot, whose grim living conditions lead them to drunken frivolity and empty amusements which enable them to endure their misery and to forget the premature approach of death and the horrors of old age: '...they died young or lived into a vile old age like their own scabby hovels' (p. 193). But the novel's main protagonists are mostly troubled. Dollbright's wife, Florence, finds she is suffering from breast cancer, whilst Bellamy Williams, son of Dollbright's workmate, suffers from unrequited love for Menna Trouncer whom he hopes will fill the place of the loving mother he never had. Menna herself vacillates, pulled between the weak young man from the flour mill and her duty to her grotesque, drunken mother, whom she has persuaded disastrously to move from Salus to Chepsford after her father had died. Just as Florence Dollbright's cancer, which she has kept secret from her husband, eats away at her from within, other characters are consumed by secret guilts: Menna regrets forcing her mother to move against her will, and wishes she had let Mrs Trouncer drink herself to death; Dollbright's lodger, Benjamin Wandby, has concealed from his landlord that he had served a prison term for the attempted murder of his sister, who also lodges with the Dollbrights.

There is no happy ending and little resolution, although there is change, even progress. Secrets are confessed, though there is no absolution. The only one made happier is Florence Dollbright, but hers is an empty victory, for, unknown to her, her operation reveals that her illness is to be fatal. She returns home full of ignorant optimism, her religious faith restored by human agency, the scalpel-wielding hand of the surgeon. Resuming worship at the Baptist chapel with new fervour, she gives foolish thanks for a non-existent recovery. Her husband, forced to abase himself before his adulterous, atheistic employer, whose life he almost envies, finally loses his faith through the very crisis which restores his wife's faith to her. Bellamy Williams and Menna Trouncer finally recognize their love for each other and spend the night together, but Menna's happiness at their long-delayed union vanishes with the dawn when she returns home to find that her mother has fallen down the cellar stairs in her drunkenness and is fatally injured. The consummation of love becomes a consummation of guilt as she realizes that having left her mother for Bellamy she has effectively killed Mrs Trouncer. She feels no guilt about sleeping with Bellamy before marrying him, only at having left her mother unguarded. Menna's choice of Bellamy depends upon the death of her mother, and her mother's earlier attempts to prevent their love affair prove that she knew that. But by her death Mrs Trouncer will blight their love and make it as intolerable as before.

Progress, therefore, often seems more circular than linear. People may experience change, losing and regaining love or religious faith, but the outcome makes little material difference, although they can never be exactly the person they were before, and change may lead to a new self-knowledge. But new understanding does not necessarily lead to greater contentment, as it seems to have done for Ifor Morriss. In fact for Dollbright or Menna it leads only to greater torment. And even love cannot bridge the void between the self and others. In fact one of the grimmest aspects of *Creed* is the isolation of characters from each other despite their living in such close proximity, their lives constantly overlapping. There are few moments of genuine warmth and human contact and, significantly, as in *Turf or Stone*, these lie outside marriage, in the honest conversation between Dollbright's employer, John Bridges, and his mistress, in the unquestioning friendship and female solidarity which Emily Jones offers Florence Dollbright in her illness, and in the short-lived happiness of Bellamy and Menna before she leaves his room for home. But these moments seem only to underline the characters' usual state of solitude, each separated from the one nearest to them by the tyranny of their particular passion and personal torment. They find it hard to share each other's burdens. Their separation from each other is often emphasized by images of dirty, whitewashed or frosted glass, through which characters may glimpse the imprecise shape of other people's lives but which prevents them from seeing each other clearly.

Although the isolation of virtually all the protagonists gives the novel a thematic unity, it also tends, again as in *Turf or Stone*, to fragment the narrative, despite the formal connections between the characters' lives. Nevertheless, the structure gains cohesion from pattern of symmetries and contrasts similiar to those Margiad Evans first used in *Country Dance*. Again characters are balanced: the Williams father and son and the Trouncer mother and daughter; the Christian married couple, the Dollbrights, and the adulterous John Bridges and his mistress. They change places like dancers, Florence Dollbright regaining her faith whilst her husband loses his; the Anglican priest paralleling the Baptist minister and, for all his dissipation, preaching a more fervent, honest creed than the nonconformist with his empty words. The death of a child in a road accident in the early part of the novel is balanced by the accidental death of the gross Mrs Trouncer at the end, the one an innocent victim, the other victim of her own vices. The inability of the characters to change their fate, even if their circumstances alter, is emphasized by the way the Mill End district is dominated by the gasworks at one end and the mill chimney at the other, not, significantly, by church tower or spire: Mill Street has a disused churchyard but no church (p.194). The theme of life dominated by toil and struggle, represented by these central images of chimney and gasworks, is reinforced by the author's semi-abstract design on the dust-jacket and title page, and by the frontispiece with its black and white design of a labouring figure. The sounds as well as the sights of industry are inescapable during daylight hours:

> The mill chimney, with its blackened top and soot-smeared brickwork, throws an angular shadow across the roofs. The streets are narrow and gritty. Here the usual sounds are the rattle of lorries as they bump over the cobbles through the double gates into the mill yard, the hissing of steam, and the churning of the engines within the square red walls, a train clanking over the iron-plate bridge, and the persistent trickle of water under the lock gate.
> (*Creed*, 17)

Florence Dollbright notices the absence of the din when she reaches hospital, where the unaccustomed silence emphasises her exile and solitude. Although the town is called Chepsford not Salus, and Salus lies some miles distant, the mill district seems to be closely based on the streets in Ross near the house in Brookend to which Mrs Whistler moved after her husband's death, and which became a base for Margiad Evans in the late 1930s. The flour mill where Bellamy Williams works and the bridge carrying the railway across the street were both local landmarks. Translated into the novel, the pounding mill and machinery take on a life of their own, in passages reminiscent of Zola. In this sense, *Creed* is Margiad Evans's *Ventre de Paris*, as she celebrates the teeming, miserable life of the working class in a small town which, like the Border in *Country Dance*, itself becomes a major protagonist in the narrative:

> Ha, what a town! What a vital, wicked, boisterous town, which beneath its vigorous life conceals a black current of despair and misery, and what people! Wild, vehement, laughing, whose two hands are generosity and vice, and whose eyes are weapons!
> (*Creed*, 22-3)

> Hanging porches were propped up by posts, hollowed steps sheered into dark holes; poisoned rats glided up and down the pavements at night looking for water, and swarmed in the drain-pipes at the side of the road which was worn and rough with flints and loosened stones. The lamps flared on the broken windows, the wind careered with rubbish in the low-roofed alleys while the people played the concertina, drank, fought and lay down on the pavements with their caps over their faces and grit in their verminous hair. The women wore their skirts hitched up in layers round their waists, and men's boots when men had done with them: their husbands showed blue dickies on a Sunday and gorgeous silk scarves instead of a collar or tie on other days. The children wore dirt and what was left over, and played such games as the law allowed outside. And all, all teemed with unabated vitality. Furtive, gnawing scraps of food, contemptuous and threatening, they peered from the cracks between the houses or shrieked across the road...
> (pp. 192-3)

Of all Margiad Evans's novels *Creed* is the one which makes the greatest demands of the reader. Although there is action, even melo-drama, this is by now less important than ideas, for it is the ideas more than the action which shape the narrative; it is the analysis of ideas which also makes it the most intellectually satisfying of her novels. More than ever before, the author takes risks. She makes no concessions to the reader who needs an easy ride in the first few pages, for although the opening paragraph is eye-catching enough with its shocking list of the parson's unparsonly doings, it is followed by a sermon occupying seven pages and then by another seven pages of theological discussion between Ifor Morriss and Francis Dollbright. This immediately sets the theme of the book, but it also demands concentration and thought from the reader.

Furthermore, narrative is distanced by the authorial interventions. Just as in *The Wooden Doctor* she reminds the reader that this is a novel, being written by the author Margiad Evans, in *Creed* she prefaces the narrative with a reminder of the presence of the author, drawing attention to the nature of the creative process and the relationship between author, text and reader. 'I begin to write, relying on the force and fine sense of each moment', are her opening words. She continues:

> The reality of my manuscript is myself translating what I have learned into scribbled words on thin paper, pinned together with ordinary pins from a pink card, while the early day shines through the blind, as through an eggshell, and the dog in the stable raves at the chink of dawn under the door.
> What I offer you as reading is real, though I outstrip each page and at the end am different.

She will not let us forget the process that lies behind the composition of the novel we are about to read, but invites us to follow her in that process. In words foreshadowing those of structuralist critics forty years later, she shows how unstable is the relationship between the writer and the text she 'translates' from experience and imagination to the manuscript page, just as the relationship between the reader and text is unstable. Writing the novel changes the author: she cannot go back to being the writer who has not yet written it, nor, of course, will the readers be unchanged after reading it. In the course of the novel the voice of Margiad Evans intervenes several times, forcibly reminding us that we are reading a novel, making us think about the relationship between writer, text and reader. In keeping with the playful, thinly disguised dedication to her sister Nancy – 'to Flo from Lil' – the tone of the author's interventions is ironic, even joky, and so alleviates momentarily, or perhaps questions, the dark mood of the narrative. In addition, just as in *Country*

Dance, there is a hint at pre-empting criticism. There she had used the introduction to justify the nature of Ann Goodman's diary; in *Creed* the tone is far more confident, humorous, but attacking, as she addresses those 'civil gentlemen in collars' who, she imagines, will disapprove of her urban subject and her treatment of it:

> I am young and the gentlemen say that when I am older I shall learn better, I shall then write of a country and its quaint customs preening themselves in old-world nooks. That will please them...
> (*Creed*, 23).

Ironically, she had already written of rural life in *Country Dance* and *Turf or Stone*, though not, of course, in any more idealized a fashion than her treatment of town life in *Creed*. And the only time the reader of *Creed* is led briefly out of the slums to the purer air of Lindenfield, the wealthy residential district, it is to witness Florence Dollbright's stressful interview with the doctor. And here, with an assured and glorious use of intertextuality before the term was invented, Margiad Evans brings back in a cameo role the Irish doctor of her second novel. We are left in no doubt that it is the same man:

> In Lindenfield, at this time – (a few years back) lived an Irish doctor of whom I have written before. His house was a melancholy building, square, brown and severe, with a white gate. Of the doctor himself there is now nothing more to be said than that he was kind and generous and fond of a joke, if he made it.
> (*Creed*, 60-1)

Again she displays a magnificent and confident disregard for contemporary literary convention. Curiously, Derek Savage, who in *The Withered Branch* (1950) criticized *Autobiography* for its lack of development and 'form', praised *Creed* more than any of her other novels, but because of what he saw as its scriptural character. It was the attempt to formulate and express a religious attitude to life which made this novel, he argued, 'one of the very few significant modern works of fiction'. Savage's assumption that a writer cannot be 'significant' without a framework of religious thought is obviously highly contentious and tells us more about his own religious convictions than about novels in general or *Creed* in particular, as Margiad Evans herself made abundantly clear in her letters to Savage after reading *The Withered Branch*. She did not and would not fit comfortably into any of his accepted categories, whether literary or religious.

It is possible that *Creed* appealed more to Derek Savage than her other novels because it is the least female of the four. Although there are three major women characters, Florence Dollbright, Mrs Trouncer (a drunken sister of the fat Mrs Lloyd Owen in *The Wooden Doctor*) and Menna, and a number of more minor ones, the narrative is seen mainly through the eyes of a man, Francis Dollbright, and it is his crisis of religious conscience which forms the main narrative thread, around which the other characters' strands are woven. Consequently, there is less emphasis on women's emotions and sexuality than in the earlier novels, although that theme is still there, notably in Menna Trouncer who swings between strong desire and strong dislike for her lover. She knows she is stronger than him and understands his need for a woman who will be a mother as well as lover or wife. Not for nothing does Bellamy's father refer to him as 'my baby'. Menna's relationship with Mrs Trouncer stands between her and freedom, but for all its nightmarish quality it reveals an unexpectedly supportive mother-daughter relationship, in as much as Menna hesitates to choose Bellamy if it means rejecting her mother. She seems to realize, moreover, that in caring for Bellamy instead of her mother she would only exchange one adult child for another. It is only the women who seem to communicate with each other on any level: with her unconditional kindness and understanding Emily Jones gives Florence Dollbright a far greater support than Florence's husband can give her. These women are far less egotistical than the men, for they are prepared, doubtless trained, to care.

As Margiad Evans was finishing *Creed*, the fatal illness of the fictional Florence Dollbright was parallelled by the decline of Godfrey Whistler. He was taken ill in November and died from liver failure in the early hours of Christmas Day 1935. Margiad's increasing feelings of pity and impending loss in those last weeks of her father's life are movingly recorded in her journal. To her genuine grief at his death was soon added practical worries about the future, for his pension died with him. There would be 'no more casual summers sleeping out of doors. No more trips on dark nights to the pictures. No more long sleeps and late breakfasts. When our money is finished we shall have to face life as others live it', she noted in her journal (23 January 1936). The family's financial situation was complicated by the fact that he had left no will and there was a delay whilst Mrs Whistler and Betty applied for letters of administration to wind up his estate. Straight after the funeral Margiad had gone to stay with Betty in London for ten days, trying to divert herself. She went to see her former publisher, Arthur Barker, and even dared herself to dress up in a red and blue football jersey and go to Jacob Epstein's studio to offer herself as a model. But she was not well and by February it was decided that she must have her tonsils removed. Since Betty's husband, William Pratt, was a doctor, it was arranged that she would go back to London and have the operation there. 'They came and poked at me with freakish curiosity in the hospital because I wrote books', she told her Bridstow friend Marjorie Byolin in a letter. 'I was a joke and a riddle.' The operation was performed successfully and she made a good recovery, although she was sure she had lost her singing voice and felt depressed by the cold and the 'yellow sootiness of everything' in London. She cheered herself up with the *Woman's Weekly* and a visit from David Garnett, who came to see her at Betty's flat in Kilburn. As in the case of Arthur Calder Marshall, it is illuminating to compare Margiad's contemporary reaction with the later recollections of the metropolitan man of letters.

In 1963 Garnett told Arnold Thorpe that he remembered meeting her 'intermittently' before the war. Inevitably this collector of literary women thought of her primarily in terms of her sex-appeal: 'I was attracted by her but I don't think she was by me'. Margiad had no illusions about him and his habits, for in her journal account of staying with David Garnett and his wife at Hilton Hall, their house near Huntingdon, she notes drily that she 'wondered how many young women [he] had brought to stay in the house, how often, for what?'. Curiously, Garnett thought she was 'rather under the thumb of her family', perhaps because he had first met her not on her own but with Nancy, and he may have supposed, wrongly, that she had brought Nancy with her for moral support. But his interpretation may also be a response to the close relationship between Margiad and her siblings, or perhaps he felt that she did not give him undivided attention.

In her post-tonsillectomy convalescence Margiad wrote of him to Marjorie Byolin in affectionate terms, much as she would of Robert Herring in the 1940s:

> Yesterday David Garnett called upon me in a lovely blue pin stripe suit ... The important thing *wasn't* the blue pin stripe suit but the kindness and large comforting companionability of this dear man even if he did sit down on the spare bed and Betty's clean laundered counterpane what cost two shillings at the laundry. He brought me a box of fruit ... blooming and beautiful in name and taste and a tube of Macleans and everything...

> He talked to me a lot and when I talked he stared at me with the most astonishing blue eyes, one nearly shut and the other bolting out of its socket so that I was a bit disconcerted but tried to go on as if they were a pair.

Garnett was obviously right to think he did not attract her sexually.

What is more significant about Margiad's accounts of these meetings, however, is that they prove how unimportant the London literary world was for her. Although she enjoyed being in the company of other writers and feeling that she was accepted as a writer herself, she was sufficiently self-confident not to try to be anything other than what she was. She also knew that for her London could never replace Herefordshire as a place to live and work. In this respect she stands in contrast to so many Welsh writers in English on whom London exerted a strong pull, such as Rhys Davies, Keidrych Rhys and the inevitable Dylan Thomas. Dorothy Edwards, the novelist from Glamorganshire whose work was acclaimed by Bloomsbury, was just six years older than Margiad. She had herself met David Garnett in 1929 and had lived in his household for some time in 1933 before returning unhappily to Wales, where she committed suicide in January 1934. Perhaps David Garnett, on his first encounter with Margiad, was expecting another Anglo-Welsh woman writer in the Dorothy Edwards mould. Margiad, however, was of a very different species. For Dorothy Edwards, although she was proud to be Welsh, it was important to be accepted and admired in London; Margiad had the self-knowledge to realize that the metropolitan literary life was not for her. She could and did enjoy interludes there, but she saw her literary jaunts as no more than a game, as her letters to Marjorie Byolin suggest. She even makes fun of her own unglamorous appearance: 'I have a black satin dinner dress but my chest is so flat and bony that I look like a vision of the Black Death'.

A visit to the photographers provoked a similar reaction. A 'literary photograph' was required for publicity purposes and Margiad treated the whole process as a joke. The photographer, Peter North, was 'a very tall man with a yellow face and pot belly who trimmed a thousand lamps upon my painted face and had no knowledge of the capacities of normal human anatomy, at least judging from the twisted poses he forced me to wear. I haven't seen the results but long to. The selection lies with Basil [Blackwell]. I don't know whether he'll choose the one like a stooping vulture or the Chinese dragon effect ... That's eight guineas.'

Between the operation, socializing and the photographer, her stay in London was a busy one. And she was writing too, 'toiling at a play', now apparently lost. She was planning to join Marjorie Byolin for a holiday by the sea in Dorset and left London in far better spirits. In early May 1936 she made a further breakthrough, for she travelled to Cardiff to make her first radio broadcast, reading from *Creed*, which had just been published. But gloom returned with the trauma of leaving Lavender Cottage which was sold at the end of that month. Fortunately she was able to take the opportunity to go away for a real holiday, leaving at the end of June to spend several weeks in Iceland with her friend Ruth Farr. The light, the strange volcanic northern landscape and its fishing and farming communities made a great impression on her, and she kept a detailed journal of her stay. As early as 1938 she was toying with the idea of writing these notes up, for in a letter to Gwyn Jones in November that year she wondered whether they might be suitable, if revised, for *The Welsh Review*, or perhaps form the basis of a book. In the event, neither idea came to fruition, although sometime before 1944 she drafted a story set in Iceland, called 'Jónas Jónsson's Horses'. However, her own recognition of this visit's importance to her is indicated by her use of parts of the Iceland journal for her essay 'Three Seas' which appeared in *Life and Letters Today* in 1945, and by a separate, unpublished, short manuscript which shows that she returned again to reworking the Iceland journal in the early 1950s.

When she returned home it was to face the break with Lavender Cottage and with Bridstow. This must have been traumatic in many ways, but it did force her to think more seriously about the future. There had undoubtedly been an element of drifting about her life in the previous years, even if she had seen four novels published in the space of five years. No longer able to fall back on home, she had to consider the possibilities and make a decision. By September 1936 the die was cast. She and Nancy, together with Basil Blackwell's daughter Helen, opened the Springherne Guest House.

Five
Springherne to Potacre (1936-1943)

Springherne was a large, comfortable house at Bull's Hill near Walford, only about two miles south of Ross-on-Wye, so Margiad and Nancy were on familiar ground. Together with Helen Blackwell as the third partner, the sisters had taken a three year lease of the property. The prospectus was designed by Margiad, or rather her alter ego, the artist Peggy Whistler, and included a sketch map and drawings. Springherne, the leaflet boasts, had 'central heating, electric light, 5 bedrooms and 2 bathrooms, garage for three cars'. It was set above its own orchard, garden and meadows, looking west over the Wye valley towards the Welsh hills, 'within easy reach of Symond's Yat, Tintern and Llanthony Abbeys, and four famous castles'. Terms were three guineas a week or two guineas for a long weekend (Friday to Tuesday), all inclusive. There were special terms, the prospectus added, for reading parties, hinting at the kind of clientele they hoped to attract. In the event, the literary guests were few, even though they advertised in the first issue of Keidrych Rhys's pioneering new journal *Wales* in the summer of 1937. The novelist James Hanley, then living further north at Llanfechain in Montgomeryshire, came to Springherne, but only for the day.

As time went on drawings by both Nancy and Margiad appeared on the walls of some of the rooms, including portraits by Nancy of some of the guests and imaginary subjects by her sister. Springherne was said to have a ghost, rejoicing in the name of Mrs Tripp, who might be heard about the house but never seen. Each of the three partners had a dog, and Margiad called hers Daniel Nathaniel Spaniel Smith. Other residents included a tame hen who used to wander indoors and was predictably christened Mrs Cluck. She had a son called Gregory Eggory. The car, an Austin Seven belonging to Helen Blackwell, was given the more elegant name of Althea. The hard work clearly did not detract from the partners' enjoyment of life, nor did their shaky finances. Their slim profits were whittled away by the lavish standards of the meals served, too extravagant for the moderate prices they charged their guests. After less than a year Margiad was complaining to Keidrych Rhys that business was bad. Nevertheless, her surviving letters from this period are cheerful and chaotic, full of glimpses of herself trying to keep the books she was reading out of the dripping bowl, or smoking best cigars while announcing the decease of her muse. Occasionally she illustrated her letters with wild sketches, and in one letter to Keidrych Rhys depicts herself in the starched and frilled pinafore she wore when waiting on the Springherne guests. At the end of her long, thin arm she holds up her letter to the sun to dry the ink as she has no blotting paper. Another illustrated letter showed Thomas Butcher, future brother-in-law of Helen Blackwell, retiring to bed in an attic above 'that ratbitten haunt behind the dart board', reached through a hole in the ceiling.

Apart from contributing a few book reviews to Keidrych Rhys's *Wales*, Margiad Evans was reading widely, even planning a trip to the British Museum 'for a tryst with Byron's letters', on which she would later base a play for radio. Her writing was not going well, however. Behind her joking reference to the death of her muse lay frustration and anxiety. After the publication of *Creed* she had received an advance from Basil Blackwell for another novel, and had made a start on it by the end of 1937. This time she left the townscape of Ross and turned back once more to the countryside of *Country Dance* and *Turf or Stone*. The mood was dark, gothic even. This book, which was to be called 'The Widower's Tale', haunted her till she died. The narrative, set in the 1860s or 1870s in a forest parish called Gwias Harold on the English side of the Border, is full of macabre and mysterious events. When Gwyn Jones invited her in November 1938 to contribute to *The Welsh Review*, of which he was the editor, she explained that she was under contract to finish the novel but lacked the financial independence to devote herself to it.

This 'ghost novel', as she described it, was supposed to come out the following spring if only she could get it done. Gwyn Jones suggested that she send an episode that could stand alone, to be published as a short story. After some misgivings she succeeded in reworking one strand of 'The Widower's Tale', where an old woman known as Aunt Flinty Knuckles, and supposed to be a witch, keeps a public house called the Nag's Head, popularly referred to as the Owld Hag's Head or the Black House. It is here that a visiting stranger apparently calls up the devil. Prophetically entitled 'The Black House', it was published as a short story in the first volume of *The Welsh Review* in 1939, and it gives some idea of the atmosphere of the unfinished novel.

On Gwyn Jones's advice she wrote to the BBC in Cardiff, offering to read either from *Country Dance* or 'The Widower's Tale' on the Welsh Home Service, and to her delight and trepidation received an invitation to make a radio broadcast from their Cardiff studios in early February 1939. Gwyn Jones and his wife Alice invited her to stay the night at their house. Alice was to meet her to bring her home so Margiad sent a characteristic thumbnail sketch of herself: 'I have dark brown hair and shall probably be wearing [an] ancient fur coat with a conspicuous tear in the hem where it caught on barbed wire' (9 February 1939). She must have looked just as she does in the photograph taken of her on Ross station later that same year; only the cigarette and dog are missing from the picture she sent to Alice Jones.

'The Black House' was broadcast on the BBC Welsh Home Service on 11 February, but she never managed to complete the novel from which it was taken. By the time the war came she had written a rough draft of no more than half of it, but it stayed in the back of her mind and occasionally the glimpse of a place or person brought the story suddenly into new life. One day in October 1942 the bus in which she was travelling passed some strange children and instantly she saw one of them as Fanny in 'The Widower's Tale', 'with the very look I imagined – bewitched and strange'. In the late 1940s and again in the mid 1950s she picked up the manuscript and began again, but it remained unfinished and fragmentary. Although the characters had become fully realized in her mind, the construction of the novel had always baffled her, as she noted in one of the later drafts: 'My problem was always where to begin and with whom. For the story so doubles and turns upon itself it would seem to indicate no definite beginning'.

It was during the years at Springherne that she met Michael Williams, the man she was later to marry and to describe as 'the dear companion of my faulty nature and physique' (*Autobiography*, 34). Writing to him in April 1945 she recalled the vivid image she had of him in those days: 'the turn of the back of your head and your hair ... like I saw you often in the orchard at Springherne, half lost & half aware.' His parents came from Fishguard in north Pembrokeshire, and were both of seafaring stock: 'a sea tribe, their weight on the waters. Even the aunts with one foot afloat' (*Autobiography*, 85). Michael's father, the Reverend Thomas Mendus Williams, had himself gone to sea in his youth, but later became a nonconformist minister before retraining as an Anglican priest. He had been a curate in the poverty-stricken industrial areas of Aberdare and Jarrow before moving in 1910 to greener pastures in Gloucestershire and Herefordshire. In 1934 he was appointed vicar at the parish church of Walford, only a mile from Springherne as the crow flies. Both the Reverend Williams and his wife spoke Welsh as their first language, but English had become the language of the home, partly because they were now living permanently in England. Many respectable Welsh families of that period, in Wales and elsewhere, were making the same choice, however, for English was considered more refined, and important for 'getting on in the world'. The three children, Hilda, Bernard and Michael, often heard their parents speaking Welsh to each other, and so understood it but did not themselves speak it fluently. Michael and Hilda often visited Margiad, Nancy and Helen at the guest house, but their brother Bernard was away from home at this time and did not meet his future sister-in-law until later.

Since the three-year lease on Springherne came to an end in September 1939 just as the war broke out, and the three women's financial situation was precarious, there could be no question of renewal. Once again Margiad faced an uncertain future. The next twelve months were filled with a series of unskilled, low-paid jobs.

'I can do everything but make a cheese soufflé', she had boasted to Thomas Butcher, but there was no call for soufflés now. After Springherne, it was not easy to adjust to being an employee again, and life as a skivvy could be hard in more ways than one. Her first job, as a housekeeper, took her far away from home, to Rampisham in Dorset, in itself a penance. 'Now I feel really homeless', she wrote in her journal that autumn. 'I am outcast from my country'. Her employers were two pious, cheeseparing spinster sisters whom she soon came to detest. 'Since Mademoiselle La Directrice [in *The Wooden Doctor*]', she wrote to Thomas Butcher, 'I've never met another monster like Miss Mary Pulleyblank – sub mentality, gray rat looks, bully, coward and mean to mania.' Springherne seemed like a distant dream: 'My God chaps was there ever a Springherne, and if there is a God why didn't he let me die on the way?' After three months she could stand it no longer, and when one of the sisters tried to place petty obstacles between her and her writing she gave notice. 'On Saturday I go but my nerve's almost broken – mine!' she told Thomas. She found another job, again in Dorset, this time at Evershott, but was consumed by homesickness. 'Oh my heart never stops its loud outcry for home, for the hills that swell suddenly in the fields', reads one of her rough notes from this time.

She returned to Ross and spent Christmas with her mother, who was now living with a friend, Miss Smith, at 17 Brookend, next to the Friends' Meeting House. This house is evoked in both *Autobiography* and the short story 'The Lost Fisherman', where it appears as the house where Emily and her mother live:

> ... at the bottom of the town near the Co-operative Mill. It had stood for centuries and smelled of stone and mice and coal, and the spicy old beams which still had the bark on some of them. It was said to be the oldest house in the town. The street door had a large dented brass knob: when you turned it and stepped into the passage it was as if you came under the shadow of a great cliff, for all the sunlight was at the back where it fell into a tiny paved yard as into a box. A long narrow corridor of a path led past a wall with a fine flat vine, as ancient as the building, to a large plot of garden. Next to that was the Friends' graveyard which had in the middle a cedar tree. This enormous geni, so dark as to be nearly black, seemed dead to all sunshine and

> looked the same by moonlight as by day. The house was simply number 17, but to the older spirits of the town it was known by its disused and genial name of The Friends' House.
> (*The Old and the Young*, 78)

This house, where her mother lived for a number of years, was the nearest thing to a base Margiad had at this time. She liked the surroundings, but felt unsettled and unhappy, though determined to write. 'Here I am where I began The Widower two years ago', she wrote in her journal, 'and where I hope to end it if this year doesn't break my heart. I will do everything just as I used: put the lamp on the kitchen table, bolt the back door' (*Autobiography*, 12). But even these rituals did not help her to finish the novel, and it was easier to 'knit and mope inwardly'. The unfinished manuscript haunted her. 'I felt my slavery, my ignominy, my dependence, my pauperhood' (*Autobiography*, 25). Nevertheless, it was not a fruitless time, for she worked regularly at what was to become the 'Winter Journal' which forms the second section of *Autobiography*. But she still felt she was making little real progress. 'Even when I have time I can't settle to anything', she told Gwyn Jones in April 1940, and the writing was only one of her problems. 'Life is treating me like hell', she added, 'and has done for the last four months.'

That spring she took a succession of jobs as a 'temp'ry slavey' in Gloucester, and this went some way to solving the problems of pauperhood and dependence, though none of her posts lasted long. She described her life in resolutely cheerful letters to Thomas Butcher: 'Many's the sink I've swilled and many's the cup I've broke ... One two three four jobs', returning between them to the nice lady in the agency who 'drinks tea and washes her daughter's stockings between interviewing titles'. Fortunately Margiad was able to take with her Gladys, her beloved spaniel, successor to Daniel and Griselda, and would arrive at each post with 'one dog basket one suitcase'. In the early summer of 1940 she worked briefly at an ordnance factory. 'I hardly know what I am', she wrote in May that year: 'Some days I am Margiad Evans, some days I find myself poking round dynamite sheds escorted by policemen'. In June she left behind her lice-filled factory overalls and went to work for the Assistance Board in Hereford, dealing with pensions. Even as a child at Benhall she was aware of poverty, and she had evoked some of its aspects in *Creed*, but now she saw it with maturer eyes 'after two months' constant rubbing up against it'. The experience put her own financial situation into perspective and gave her an overwhelming respect for the very poor.

New worries came in June 1940 when she heard that her brother Roger, who was in the army, had been posted missing, although later the family heard that he was safe but taken prisoner of war. Yet there were light-hearted moments too, riding her bicycle into the river 'to see what it was like riding a bicycle in pink French knickers into a river and it was lovely', living with an eccentric old lady in 'the sort of house where the ink bottle turns up in the apple pie holding up the crust', as she described it to Thomas Butcher that September. 'The room is furnished with a grand piano, a chair and clusters of jam jars full of mouldy plums and stagnant water sitting on the floor ... I play "Jerusalem the Golden" on the piano and "I Dreamed I Dwelled in Marble Halls". The music seems to flitter out of the cracks of the lid – it sounds faint and eerie, harp-like'. Music was still an important element in her life and she and her mother composed a marching song, Mrs Whistler writing the music and her daughter the words. A music publisher accepted it but wanted them to make a contribution to his costs, so the venture came to nothing.

After leaving Springherne, Margiad Evans had kept in close touch with Michael Williams. They were able to meet regularly while she was based at Brookend, and their long walks in the countryside around Ross are reflected in the early sections of *Autobiography*. By the summer of 1940, however, while Margiad was living in Hereford, Michael Williams was working on a farm at Brickhampton, near Cheltenham, thirty miles away. In peacetime the distance would not have been too great, but wartime conditions of travel and long working hours made it hard for them to see each other as often. But they met when they could and wrote to each other and by late August 1940, after some uncertainty, they decided to marry 'one fine day when our courage is at boiling point', as she told Thomas Butcher. 'Nobody's allowed to come to our absurd wedding. It will take place with a lot of wrangling and end in a picnic with a pork pie. [Mike] never stops working and I shall start cooking the dinner straightaway'. They were married quietly in Gloucester on 28 October and started their life together at Brickhampton in a tiny rented cottage. The following January, however, they moved in to a cottage called Potacre in Llangarron, a village about five miles south-west of Ross-on-Wye and only about three miles from the Border. Potacre was to be her home for the next seven years, first of all with her husband and then, after he was called up, increasingly alone. Despite the sadness and worry his absence brought her, and the grinding exhaustion brought by year after year of war and poverty, these years at Llangarron inspired some of her finest and most mature writing.

The house was one of two semi-detached cottages on top of the hill a few hundred years above Llangarron church. It had a garden where they could grow fruit and vegetables and keep bees, and an outside 'Elsan' lavatory which they christened Elsie. Margiad's constant companions would be her beloved spaniel, Gladys, later succeeded by Rosie, and a greedy, sybaritic cat, Thomas Catto, who plays a cameo role in *Autobiography*. Next door lived Mr and Mrs Saunders, whom she referred to privately as Peg-leg and Ellen. Ellen Saunders became a kind and thoughtful friend, keeping an eye on Margiad while Mike was away in the forces, lending a hand and bringing her eggs or other produce. Her drawback was her fondness for chatting. Like many of the other neighbours, she could not understand that Margiad, despite her own keen appetite for gossip, often needed periods of peace and solitude for meditation and writing. As a result, the writing often had to be done late at night, after Margiad had heard through the party-wall the thump of Peg-leg's wooden leg on the stairs as he stumped up to bed. 'I hope I don't revert to the nights when I never slept but wrote and drank black coffee and smoked cigars', she wrote to her husband in July 1942. That had been possible when she had no other work pressing. But now, apart from housekeeping, chopping firewood, gardening and bee-keeping, she was often taking casual labouring work on farms, beet-hoeing, pulling beet, lifting potatoes or apple-picking, and she could not afford to burn the candle both ends.

Apart from Ellen Saunders she made other good friends at Llangarron, notably Margaret Scudamore who lived at a farm called

Panbrook. She was a sensible, intelligent woman, whose well-to-do farmer husband, like Margiad's brother Roger, became a prisoner of war. Margaret was a great ally but never intruded and provided just the kind of unpossessive friendship Margiad appreciated. After one afternoon spent with Margaret she wrote in her journal: 'We talked of many things and I felt running between us the secret communication of two minds that are very much alike' (5 July 1944). It was a great loss to her when Margaret and her family moved away in 1947. To the people of Llangarron Margiad must have seemed a very unconventional person. To be a woman writer was unusual enough, but she looked different too, as another neighbour, Eva Trevor, explained to Arnold Thorpe: 'Her dress was always eccentric and sometimes she had her hair in two plaits, loose or done on top, and trousers tied up with string half way up the legs and a scarf round her neck. But she got away with it, looking quite picturesque.'

Llangarron was near enough for Margiad Evans to see relatives and old friends living in the Ross area, including her mother, her parents-in-law and Michael's sister Hilda. Her own sisters visited from time to time during the war, as did her old friend Ruth Farr. Sometimes she escaped to London for a few days, staying with another woman friend, Joey Hodgkinson, whom she had met at Llangarron and whose baby's grave in Llangarron churchyard Margiad kept tidy. In London she was able to dip her toe once more into literary life, meeting on one of these visits Robert Herring, editor of *Life and Letters To-day*, who regularly published work by her during the 1940s. She first met him for tea at his house in Chelsea and was impressed by how domestic he was. 'He does all his own work, even the mangling!' she reported to her husband (7 July 1945). Like her, she noted, Herring had to attend to domestic and other duties by day and wrote at night.

The war years at Llangarron are extremely well documented by two major sources. In March 1941 she started keeping a journal again, after allowing the habit to lapse during the first months of her marriage, and it was these resumed journals which became the basis of the later sections of *Autobiography*. But her letters to her husband are even more informative. When Michael Williams was first called up to the forces he was based in Britain, and there were times when he could come home for the weekend or she could pay him a brief visit. Once he was posted abroad, however, and spent the rest of the war on board ship in the Mediterranean, Margiad lived alone month after month. To maintain not only the link between them but also the reality of their home for him, she wrote to him virtually every day. These letters, of which hundreds survive, were written in snatched moments late at night or early morning and it was these which now formed her fullest journal. She even described them in such terms: 'This simple journal for Mike' she wrote at the head of one of the first letters she sent him after he joined up (13 July 1942). Separate notebooks and journals survive, kept from May 1942 onwards, but their content is often fragmentary or discontinuous.

Her journal-letters, often illustrated with sketches, provide a wealth of information about her activities, thoughts and feelings, and she recognized that 'whoever I am writing to, it is really always to myself'(journal, 13 October 1942). For Michael and herself she recorded the minutiae of her days and nights, impressions of the sights, sounds, smells and feel of the countryside through its changing seasons. Like many women's letters to men in the forces at this time, they also document life on the Home Front: rumours about the progress of the war and accounts of air-raids, the arrival and departure of evacuees, new rules and regulations, especially with regard to employment and agriculture, and the pressure to participate in the 'war effort' in a thousand trivial ways. In the summer of 1942 there was worrying talk about childless women between the ages of eighteen and forty-five being called up, although Margiad hoped that her work on the land would exempt her. Then came the fear that, living alone, she would have an evacuee foisted on her, or a landgirl as a lodger, which would interfere with her writing. In 1945, when she was already deeply upset at the death of her beloved dog Gladys from distemper, she felt reproached by some of her neighbours for not working and contributing to the war effort as much as she should, although nothing seems to have come of her attempts to find regular part-time work. Her letters often express these stresses on her as well as the sadness of separation from her husband, and her worries for his safety once he was sent abroad on active service in 1944. Manual work brought fatigue and backache and she also still had painful bouts of cystitis. Nevertheless, her letters are not all gloom, for they reflect her enjoyment of the beauties of the country-side and a hundred simple pleasures in her daily life. They are also enlivened with gossip, often recounted in the exact words of the speaker, so that conversations and personalities leap vividly from the page. Like *Country Dance*, these letters, which of course were written only for her husband's private reading while they were apart, enable us to peep through a keyhole into another life.

In many ways these letters can also be seen as literary work-books, and point to the continuum that always existed between her daily life and her art. The discipline of regular observation followed by an attempt to convey her experiences and impressions in words helped the writer in her to survive. It is not surprising that many of the small incidents which later found their way into stories or essays can be traced back to this correspondence. Some letters contain ideas for stories or even detailed outlines or early drafts of work that was later polished up and completed. The letters also enable us to date fairly accurately most of the short stories and essays and some of the poems she was working on during the war years, for she usu-ally reports on their progress.

Despite her circumstances, the literary output of these years was of remarkable quality and originality. The gap of seven years between the publication of *Creed* and of *Autobiography* had seen great changes in her life and those changes are reflected in her new work. In *The Withered Branch* Derek Savage pointed to those seven years of apparent silence as 'significant in her deterioration as a writer', arguing that she had written herself into a dead-end. He could not have been further from the truth. To correct his false con-clusions, Margiad Evans wrote to Savage in March 1950 to point out that in those years the sale of her parents' house had left her with-out a home, she had been forced to take jobs here and there at low salaries, and was therefore unable, by force of circumstances, to fin-ish 'The Widower's Tale' which she owed Blackwell in return for the advance he had paid her long since. 'Even the Brontës', she added, 'had a maid and a home and a centre!' She explained that she offered *Autobiography* instead of 'The Widower's Tale' to Blackwell, to clear the debt which she had no other means of paying off. But if 'poverty and the inability to buy privacy to write in' had been a major factor in her failure to finish the novel, the existence of *Autobiography* shows that she was still writing well. The great advantage of the journal form was that she could write in whatever quiet and undisturbed moments presented themselves. Like many women writers before and since, she could not write full time but had to confine her writing to time stolen from labour in house, garden and the fields. 'The joys of *Autobiography* were snatched moments from the type of life lived by any poor woman without help', as she explained to Derek Savage. 'If you notice you will see that many of the things witnessed in it were seen while fetching water, mending a sheet or a shirt etc.' The need to fit her writing around other work became increasingly pressing as the war began to impose ever greater burdens on women.

The journals which make up the thirteen sections of *Autobiography* were originally written between early 1939 and early 1943, but comparison with original drafts, where this is possible, shows that they were extensively revised. Some of those sections were first published separately in *Life and Letters* in 1940 and 1941, but in January 1941 she told Robert Herring that she was thinking of bringing them together for publication as a volume, to be illustrated with a series of her own watercolours. Wartime restrictions and the high cost of printing unfortunately reduced the proposed series of coloured illustrations to one black and white frontispiece when *Autobiography* appeared in 1943.

The arrangement of the thirteen sections of *Autobiography* is only roughly chronological and its title is misleading to the unwary, for it is not an autobiography in the usual sense of the word. It is very little concerned with narrating the external detail of her life, and covers only four years. At first sight, moreover, it may seem more of a nature diary, in the tradition of Gilbert White's *The Natural History of Selborne*. Yet it is intensely autobiographical, being based on extracts from actual journals. Hence her descriptions of the natural world and her meditations on it have their starting point in everyday tasks:

> Washed kitchen, larder and parlour floors. Cooked, hung out
> clothes. Heard the plovers and the wind intermingled. The wind

feels its strength and barrenness. Picked up sticks. The heifer in the stream, head down, hind legs up on the bank drinking the light in the water. Sunlight in the afternoon and the great branches suspended over the golden ground. The oak leaves lie with edges up, too quiet to glitter; then a gust, and look, myriads of scampering mice they seem, or fledglings hopping and flying.

I got up at quarter to six. When M– was gone I went to the door and lifted the latch and listened. The plovers were awake and wheeling but the rooks making a sleepy nestling sound under the hill. Down there it was darker. Blackbirds in the hedge. I went and fetched a fork. The shed let light in through the tiles and under the eaves revealing the belly of the roof. So softly, slyly the morning came without a sunrise. It was still until about midday when the wind came flooding the field like a river rushing back along a dried channel. It hit me as I stood on the path looking down at the shadows that had been so quiet but now seemed trying to fly away from the ground. The movement seemed to be *under* them – almost as if the garden itself were quaking and bursting with some strange sudden growth.

(*Autobiography*, 77)

But above all the book is autobiographical because it provides a descriptive analysis of the writer's internal life: 'the record of my gravest (that is happiest) inner existence' (*Autobiography*, 150). In this respect it has some affinity with *The Wooden Doctor*, where the external events in Arabella's life are set in the perspective of her emotional turmoil. With its emphasis on the spiritual aspect of the writer's life, however, it recalls far more the now much-maligned autobiographies and biographies of nineteenth-century Welsh preachers, which concentrate on the individual's spiritual journey through life, usually neglecting to record external events such as marriage, birth of children and the like. It is the chronicling of Margiad Evans's spiritual progress which gives *Autobiography* its shape and internal logic, and that development takes place through living almost exclusively in relation to the natural world with its changing seasons.

She begins in a state of uncertainty out of which emerges her first attempt to make sense of the world and her relationship to it, an important step, which is facilitated by the rediscovery of herself and of childhood vision. Although a child can only perceive the world in terms of its own self, trying to put itself into what it sees, it has insights which adults have usually lost. These can be retrieved, for 'things in childhood which were not childish are permanent'. Furthermore, 'visions in childhood have childish form but they are not childish in themselves' (*Autobiography*, 149), so the adult can learn anew that way of seeing and benefit from it. In this way Margiad Evans gains new understanding of the natural world around her and her relationship to it. Initially this makes her all too conscious of the problem of communication. She cannot comprehend the language of beasts and birds, nor they hers, even though they are part of the same world, but some kind of intuitive knowledge and understanding can be achieved through the close, careful observation that is only possible by forgetting or losing the self. 'As nothing individual I go out. Lapsing and losing myself I seem to breathe through distant trees ... I discard my particularity ...' (p. 103).

The greatest difficulty then is to convey to other human beings, her 'bodily thoughts', for 'what I see I don't see with my eyes alone', particularly because this demands that a transitory perception be 'translated to permanent wording' (p. 49). She experiments with poetry as a medium for evoking for others at least the mood or feeling she experienced, but she was conscious that the examples she included in *Autobiography* 'move only in me' (pp. 6-7). In the foreword to *Creed* she had written of 'translating what I have learned into scribbled words on thin paper', a concept she now develops in a different context, as she grapples with the problem of describing in language perceptions experienced in non-linguistic terms: 'I think in a language I cannot speak, and the sounds I hear often speak to my thoughts in the same untranslatable idiom' (p. 117). Later she would extend this idea still further, describing all forms of art as translation: 'Its native language is known only – felt and heard only – by its creator. The hearers of music hear the executant's translation of the creator's mother tongue' (journal, 14 April 1948). Although in *Autobiography* she is determined to 'try to write for people who feel and understand' the natural world around them (p. 111), there is always a 'loss of *something* which no pondering and no effort can bring back' (p. 48). In the end, however, this concern is overcome by the sheer joy of the revelation of a spiritual 'continuity, the connection between all living things' (p. 92), which for her provides the key to understanding. Nature is never static, yet it is always the same: 'All, all in sight and hearing was Nature pouring itself from one thing into another, spending and creating, running like the wind over the body of life, and flowing like blood through its heart. All changed, and nothing changed' (p. 93). Her knowledge that she too is part of this continuity, this merging of all existences, becomes the essential truth of her own life, far more important than external events, and so her book is the truest kind of autobiography:

> If I may keep this knowledge, this perpetual life in me, anybody may have my visible life; anybody may have my work, my smile, if I may go on sensing the thread that ties me to the sun, to the roots of the trees and the springs of joys, the one and separate strand to each star of each great constellation.
> (*Autobiography*, 93)

Autobiography reveals a major change in her writing since the publication of *Creed*, a change that seems to come from within herself, which suggests that in explaining the seven years' gap to Derek Savage she did not tell the whole story. In her novels she had concentrated on the study of human beings, on individuals and their feelings and relationships. The main protagonists of those novels are egotistic and thus essentially child-like, especially from *The Wooden Doctor* onwards. With the self-centredness of children they want to be the hub of their particular universe, and so have little regard for the feelings of others or understanding of them. Thus they may inflict emotional, mental or physical pain on others with little compunction. In *Autobiography*, personal as it is, her attention is now less on the self, or on other people, than on the natural world, and in meditating on her own relationship to that world she writes not so much as a distinctive personality but as a representative of humankind, hence her insistence on the need to forget the self. In retrospect, a process of gradual maturing can be traced in the three last novels, from the closely autobiographical *The Wooden Doctor*, where she becomes her own flawed heroine and spokeswoman, to the broader range of characters and viewpoints in *Turf or Stone* and especially *Creed*. From what is known of her life when these were written, it is fair to conclude that in many ways those three novels are narratives of her own psyche. The death of her father, the change in her material circumstances after the sale of Lavender Cottage, the coming of the Second World War and above all the development of her relationship with Michael Williams, seem to have brought about a process of emotional and psychological maturing which had been delayed.

Perhaps the most important factor in this process, turning her eyes outward rather than inward on herself, was her love for her husband. He emerges from both her public, published work and her private letters to him, as a true partner, someone with whom she felt a profound and shared understanding, hence his important presence in *Autobiography*. There she describes him as someone who 'thinks from inside Nature', who does not disturb her necessary sense of solitude in the country. It infuriates her 'that people cannot see one alone without charging into conversation' (*Autobiography*, 82), but in his presence the meditation she associated with solitude can thrive. 'In some strange way', she felt, '[he] resembles solitude ... he is a part of myself ... at some moments ... we are blended in our surroundings, more than brother and sister, nearer than lovers, deeper and more unconscious than our separate selves' (p. 73). Through her relationship with him she felt that she had rediscovered her lost self: 'Living with M– has let me find myself entirely, let me go back, never I hope to be lost again, in that blind crowding' (p. 81). This feeling is reiterated in her letters to him. 'Oh my dear dear young man', she wrote in January 1943, 'what a restoration our marriage has been to me!' She could now retrieve her childhood awareness of nature, and feel again that continuity of life between herself and the natural world: 'once more like a child ... but only because this time is as *that* time. No going back but a long way forward – *nearer* to this resemblance' (*Autobiography*, 82). The negative feelings which tortured her in the mid 1930s – a sense of isolation and bitterness, coupled with self-pity, resentment, dissatisfaction – fade away, and she emerges soothed, calmed, made whole.

Linked with this change is a new awareness of the divine. If the novels were concrete, rooted in human society and its material culture, *Autobiography* is above all spiritual and mystical. And whereas

Turf or Stone or *Creed* depict a world devoid of true knowledge of God, and characters to whom God is not revealed, or who rage against him, in *Autobiography* Margiad Evans happily acknowledges God. As she had predicted, to know God she had had to pass through the stage of unbelief. 'No more resentment. No more passion or complaint, tears or justification. No more grief and pain and betrayal. Only joy. *Thou* Father knowest me.... God be between us all like the lovely air' (*Autobiography*, 10). He is not, however, a conventional Christian God, and Christ has no place in her religious consciousness now or in any of her work. In fact the Christian concept of redemption through sacrifice and washing in the blood of the lamb seemed to her appalling. 'I am not a scrap religious – entirely indifferent to creeds and Christians', she wrote to the newly widowed Kate Roberts in November 1946. She loathed sermons and addresses, and would not go to church because she was 'a believing unbeliever', she added. Her need for solitude is explicitly linked with her new acceptance of God. 'Of course you are lonely', she told Kate Roberts, 'but don't fear it – everything durable, everything eternal comes out of loneliness ... I think that loneliness trains one for death – for life too – and that when you are away from people you are with God. Her belief that 'all life whatever [is] a oneness' (*Autobiography*, 154) makes her aware of her own smallness and insignificance, but if she is no more important than a leaf or an ant, paradoxically she can be important for being part of the living and dead in the natural world. She cannot accept a difference, or at least a gulf between 'a *human* nature and a universal nature'. This idea is explored in her letters to Michael Williams at this time, as she sought to find a way of expressing in words what she felt:

> Sometimes I feel filled with a profound and joyful certainty. I don't know what it is, I don't even care. I only know it is there. In the same way that Eternity is in the stream water, in the dew and the stars and on the misty hills, embodied in flickering, animate in the near, the remote, the one ceaseless continuation is in my heart. It's a thought and yet not so much a thought as an eye looking into an eye.
> (9-10 September 1942)

The idea of the soul as a peculiarly human prerogative, the badge of human superiority over the animal and plant worlds, thus becomes an irrelevance to her, and she is able to accept happily her own smallness within the universe. What Derek Savage discerned as a 'death-wish' in her writing is in fact an attempt to understand the mystery of mortality and a calm acceptance of death as a natural, integral part of life.

In its exploration of the relationship between the human being and the natural world and in its celebration of personal faith in some divine impulse within nature, *Autobiography* stands within a literary tradition exemplified in the works of two of Margiad's favourite authors, the American Henry David Thoreau and the Englishman Richard Jefferies. But although she found their writing inspiring, neither influenced her work directly. She shared with Thoreau the experience of living a life in close harmony with nature, which he celebrated in *Walden*, as well as his belief in the importance of solitude and forgetting the self. In her close observation of nature, focusing ever more closely on a particular detail – the turn of a leaf, the quality of a ray of sunlight – and in the elated spiritual awareness that she gains from this process, or the sense of the oneness of the natural world, she has much in common with Jefferies:

> By me the olive-smooth seed case of the field poppy is balanced on its bare stem. I can feel its weight, see the black crest, like a seal, that shuts in the seeds, touch its smooth cold surface. It is like a deserted bird's egg, so heavy and cold in the hand. At the same time I see in me the hidden seeds in their pearly rows under the yellow olive skin, and the perfect flower all silky red and purple, tossing flimsily with the ripening oats. The actual thing I touch is not more real than the flower in me. The stubble glinting, the nettles bending are no closer than the sudden vision of the sword grass, seen so clearly, so distinctly, down to the sharp central crease which folds it to a point. I often feel as I walk by the trees that I see their roots with its grubs asleep in the earth, and the shiny chrysalis embedded in the rotten stump. Through all the connection flows onward, inward, outward, flowing life of thought, of sun and moon, of bone, and core and vision. As the stars are in the sky in daylight, as the sun is under the darkness, always in the sky, the eternal connection binds the universe, the transferring force passes forever from one life to another, from one form to another.
> (*Autobiography*, 92)

But whereas for Jefferies the process ended in a hopeless conviction of the absence of God, for her, as we have seen, his existence is revealed through Nature. Moreover, whereas Jefferies recalls an idealized country where he was born and brought up and from which he was exiled in adult life, Margiad Evans was born 'exiled' from her true country, which she did not glimpse until she was nine years old, and she did not live there until she was eleven. When writing the journals on which *Autobiography* is based she had had to leave Bridstow, but she was still living in the same area, seeing the same hills, and, again unlike Jefferies, she needed to be in her own country to be able to write about it. A woman's relationship with home is probably different from a man's: whereas Jefferies and many other male writers such as John Cowper Powys only wrote of the place in which they grew up when they were exiled from it, it is striking how many women writers, from Jane Austen and the Brontës to Mary Webb and Phyllis Bentley, have written about their home area from within it.

Neither does Margiad Evans share the strongly elegiac mood of Jefferies's work, for she accepts that childhood must end. What is important to her is that she has been able to retrieve from childhood significant memories and the child's visionary way of seeing. It is true that like Jefferies (and indeed Thoreau) she expresses a strong preference for traditional country life as opposed to town and the shift to industrial work, a theme introduced in *Creed* and touched on in *Autobiography*:

> In nature there's no unsatisfiable craving to match civilization's horrible predatory attitude towards 'the next job'. It cannot be virtue to make incessant industry the rhythm and thought of existence. Besides, few modern people ever see the beginning and end of their work ... they are the middle, or the finish or the idea.
>
> (*Autobiography*, 36)

But this does not lead her to share Jefferies's nostalgia and bitterness at this change, with its political implications, and in the end she appears almost indifferent to urban life as something which was irrelevant to her. Although she celebrates work on the land, perceiving the spiritual dimension of labour on the land as part of a changeless rhythm and harmony, there is no socio-political agenda in *Autobiography*, and in the end a specific landscape is more important to her than the specific human community in which she lives. She may regret the changes brought by mechanization but accepts them. Writing to Kate Roberts in 1952 she agreed that they had both witnessed the disappearance of their 'childhood world' with its 'horses and traps, lanterns, white lanes, sunbonnets and wooden hayrakes like combs', but added 'I see nothing so interesting now but I suppose if I were a child I should'. She realized that a child and its later adult self will always see its own time as the best.

Although Margiad Evans may have affinities with Thoreau, Jefferies and other writers inspired by a particular landscape and the natural world within it, in many respects her work and outlook are very different from theirs. Hers is, of course, a woman's eye, and so she often uses images drawn from specifically female experience to convey meaning, describing a newly harrowed field, for instance, 'as if knitted in a smaller stitch' (*Autobiography*, 81), and ants in a disturbed nest rescuing their nymphs as 'smallish-sized landladies' struggling with 'double-bed bolsters' (p. 130). What she has in common with those earlier male writers is a close observation of the natural world and meditation upon it, which leads to a deeper understanding and even to revelation. Form and style followed from that experience, not from direct literary influence. Although *Autobiography* is a highly personal work, written out of herself and for herself, that self is seen not as an individual of particular significance but as a representative human being concerned with questions about life itself. Moreover, her experience is not limited by a particular time, place or specific human community. As a result, after more than half a century of tremendous change in the countryside, *Autobiography* has not dated nor lost its ability to strike a chord in the reader.

Six

Flowers under Fallen Leaves:
Poetry and Prose (1943-1948)

Journal-writing and letter-writing were not the only literary occupations that Margiad Evans succeeded in slotting in to stray corners of time between house, garden and field during the war and in the years that followed. Poetry, essays and short stories gradually emerged. She often felt progress was slow but in the circumstances her output was remarkable. Much of it was also published, earning her far better pay than farm work. In late July 1942, after collecting ten shillings as wages for beet-hoeing, she noted that during the month she had so far earned £2.1s.8d. at that work, and 7s.7d. from selling honey, but Robert Herring would pay her up to eight pounds for a story or essay published in *Life and Letters*. Herring was also asking her to review books, as was Gwyn Jones, editor of *The Welsh Review*, and this again helped to supplement her husband's low salary and her own tiny income, sometimes by a guinea or as much as two pounds. *Autobiography* sold steadily too, despite mixed reviews: in November 1944 Margiad Evans reported to her husband that a woman she knew in Ross had just bought the last copy in Smith's for a Christmas present, 'so I shall have ninepence at least to play with'.

For the first time she was having poems published as well as prose. To compose poetry was not a new departure for her, for from as early as the mid 1930s her journals include drafts of verse, and six such poems, composed in 1939 and 1942, had been included in *Autobiography*. In that context poetry provided another way of conveying in words a meaning sometimes beyond ordinary words, but it had other advantages too. Poetry is the ideal form for the working woman engaged in physical labour, for it can be first drafted in the mind, the repeated movements of washing, digging or hoeing providing a strong background rhythm to the patterning of words. It is not surprising, therefore, that Margiad Evans sometimes refers in her letters and journals to lines forming in her mind in this very way. Sometimes they presented themselves with such urgency that she felt compelled to drop what she was doing and grab paper and pen to set the poem down quickly before it escaped.

It is appropriate, too, that the first poem published independently should reflect the harsh reality of women's lives in rural poverty. She described 'The Passionate Refusal' as 'a practical retort' to Christopher Marlowe's well-known poem, 'The Passionate Shepherd to his Love', firmly rejecting Marlowe's pastoral ideal:

> I would not lead so hard a life,
> She said, to be a labourer's wife.
> To serve with love and gravy feasts
> My husband, slogman to the beasts.
>
> To share his hands with cattle hide,
> And lie down on the bed beside
> The form of him who spread the straw
> For pigs and cows to dung the floor.
>
> To gather sticks with soap-soaked hands
> Creeping like toads on rich men's lands –
> Our only treasure be what's thrown
> Out from the farm, or what we'd grown –
>
> Great chilblain roots in earthy sacks
> Carried in groaning on our backs,
> Potatoes like cobbles in the dark
> Under your feet, then roasted stark
>
> With cheese for supper – and the snow!
> I don't know why I fear it so –
> I never could – I'd feel too much:
> The things I dreamed *I'd have to touch.*
>
> And oh, she said, I think I see

FLOWERS UNDER FALLEN LEAVES

Our dog that wouldn't care for me;
A hound-eared cur I'd come to hate
The one thing lower than my mate.

A creature that he'd only keep
To work, and then be kicked asleep.
I could not lead so foul a life,
She wept, to be a labourer's wife.

To darn, she said, and never tire
Of patching holes by wooden fire.
I shiver at the thought! and yet
I'd do it if I could forget
The final heavy sheet I'd mend
For our iron death-bed at the end.
                    (*Poems from Obscurity*, 13-14)

Living in Llangarron she had witnessed this life at first hand, and
her letters and journals show that she felt strongly that the price of
such labour was ignored or undervalued by society. In July 1942 she
described to Michael Williams how she had stopped for a drink of
water at a cottage where the woman 'told me she used to work in
the fields, come back home and cook and clean for eight people. [I]
wonder if it'll ever be realized what wonderfully valuable people
the working women are. They ought to have a cenotaph'. Sending
'The Passionate Refusal' to Gwyn Jones in November 1943 for publication in *The Welsh Review*, she noted the difference in tone to
Autobiography, which he had just read and praised. 'There are at
least two distinct writers in me', she explained. 'The "poem" was
written by the thump-thump one who wrote most of *Turf or Stone*.'
This dichotomy reflected 'the two sides to the country – the loveli-
ness and peace, and the brutal, human side which cannot be exag-
gerated.' Three weeks later she sent him a poem written in a very
different vein, entitled 'Resurrection':

My candle burns up lank and fair,
The gale is on the pane,
The dead leaves on the whirlwind's branch
Are risen trees again.

And can I sleep to-night, my heart,

93

With candle and with storm?
And dare I sleep, my heart, my heart,
And see my dreams alone?

For when in my resurgent hands
I take the mirror weedy with brown hair:
Rustling the dark wind through the glass –
Oh, who is there?
                    (*Poems from Obscurity*, 15)

In both mood and imagery 'Resurrection' recalls Margiad Evans's first novel, *Country Dance*. The 'mirror weedy with brown hair' recalls Ann Goodman's sight of herself in her looking-glass, and the description of Ann's dead face in the water at the end of the story, whilst the second stanza in particular is reminiscent of the folk-songs quoted and referred to in that book. But the repeated questioning creates a very different atmosphere from the inevitability of fate which hangs over Ann Goodman. *Country Dance* provided black-and-white statements with the confidence of the young writer, but now the reader is faced with ambiguity and questions to answer.

At first Margiad Evans was very diffident about these two poems. 'Is this a poem?' she asked Gwyn Jones when she sent him 'Resurrection'. He had no such doubts and accepted both for publication in *The Welsh Review*. When she saw them in print she felt more positive about them: 'I do think they stand out with a kind of bold simplicity', she told her husband. Thus encouraged, she continued to compose poetry from time to time, although sometimes 'my sparse poems make me chuckle' she told Gwyn Jones (13 December 1944). A turning point came in 1945 when she acquired a literary agent. In April that year she asked Basil Blackwell to release her from her obligation to publish with him, and in early July, while staying for a few days in London, she arranged to see the agent David Higham, on the recommendation of Robert Herring. Higham suggested she prepare a volume of verse. She thought this impossible as she had only fifteen suitable poems ready. 'But twenty would be enough, he says. So perhaps one day. I should like that,' she reported to Michael Williams (7 July 1945). By the autumn of 1946 she had more than enough for a book and in October heard from David Higham that Andrew Dakers was willing to publish it. *Poems from Obscurity*, although dated 1947, finally appeared in January 1948, with a dedication to her god-daughter, Anna, daughter of Margiad's sister Betty.

It contained thirty-six poems, of which five had been included in *Autobiography*, six published in *The Welsh Review*, two in *Life and Letters To-day* and one in *Orion*. She was not entirely happy with the book. 'It's no title', she grumbled to Gwyn Jones after the second proofs arrived, 'and I hate the look of it and why publish what nobody will like and won't make a penny I think' (23 March 1947). She was equally unenthusiastic when the published volume appeared. Her gloom arose partly from being worn down, for the years of wartime privation had given way only to further shortages and food-rationing and an even greater struggle to live. Her husband had returned to agricultural work after being demobbed in the spring of 1946 and was working long hours, so the work in the garden as well as the house tended to fall on Margiad's shoulders. Sometimes during these post-war years she felt as if she had no more to say: 'Funny to have an agent now when I am so very near my end I feel', she had mused to Gwyn Jones a year previously (6 March 1946).

Her misgivings about her *Poems from Obscurity* were not entirely groundless, for the quality is uneven. Some of the poems are too simple, owing too much, perhaps, to the influence of W.H. Davies and Walter de la Mare. Most are written in regular metre and rhyme which to the present-day ear may give them too strong a rhythm, which overshadows the words and their meaning. This can even give an impression of strain as the syntax is made to fit the metre and certain lines seem too self-consciously 'poetic', as if she had not always been able to find her own voice. At their best, however, especially where metre and rhyme are less obtrusive, these poems can be powerful, mysterious and deeply evocative.

Many of them, even the later compositions, continue themes she had developed in *Autobiography*: the continuity of all life in nature, the recurring cycle of death and rebirth which brings signs of new life in the midst of decay, like 'flowers under fallen leaves' ('There is a castle'), or the blue butterflies which flutter lightly above the heavy 'earth-lidded eyes' of the dead child in 'Lullaby to the Child in the Grave', a poem perhaps inspired by her friend Joey's baby lying in Llangarron churchyard. She returns too to the question of communication between the human being and the rest of existence, in poems such as 'Night Wind' with its image of 'The leaf which wrote upon the ground/And there left signed/A word that none will read for evermore'. The related problem of recovering, and so communicating with, the self as child is considered here as it was in *Autobiography*, notably in 'Children', where it is now associated with a sense of loss:

> ... A moment ago I was with them,
> A moment ago I was one.
>
> The shrill of my childhood's language
> Beats round their heads like birds –
> They have taken my country from me
> They have beckoned my singing words.

Death is another recurrent theme, sometimes overtly, as in 'Death (Song of a Cage-bird)', where the shared mortality of bird and human is stressed by the repeated, heavy refrain 'I must die too ... I must go too', whilst the idea of the cage through which the bird's soul slips recalls the death of Shanlea, the bird-cage maker, at the end of her early, unpublished 'Fairy Story'. For the countrywoman in 'The Passionate Refusal' a life of toil would be rewarded only by 'our iron death-bed at the end', whilst 'Town Walk' with its streets 'simple as graves' is full of images of death. In other poems mortality is less overt but still present, suggested by the emphasis on transitoriness of time, on night and separation from light ('The Vision', 'Age'), and on sleep in the two 'Lullabies', or by images of rain-sodden vegetation. In 'There is a Castle', based on memories of her stay at Loches in her teens, the flag 'Waving behind, good-bye, good rest' and the Hardyesque image of the locked, neglected garden create a similarly elegiac mood, although, characteristically, Margiad Evans introduces in the final stanza a reminder of new life reborn under the decay.

Such paradoxes and contrasts abound in *Poems from Obscurity*, whether in the sudden quiet after bank holiday crowds have gone home, or in the frequent juxtaposition of light and darkness, stillness

1. Nancy, Betty and Peggy Whistler, Ross, 1920

2. Coch-y-bûg, Pontllyfni, c.1965

3. Cours Saint-Denis, Loches, c.1925

4. Nancy, Betty and Peggy Whistler with their mother at Lavender Cottage, Bridstow, 1936

6. Sketch
by Peggy
Whistler
for the
Springherne
prospectus,
late 1936

5. The Mill,
Brookend,
Ross, c.1965

7. Margiad Evans with her dog, Gladys, on Ross station, late 1939

8. Friends'
House,
Brookend,
Ross, c.1965

9. Margiad Evans and Michael Williams in the Black House, Elkstone, 1952

10. Margiad Evans with her daughter Cassandra Williams, and her dog Rosie, Cheltenham, c.1953

and movement, old age and youth, or physical and spiritual existence. The last is often suggested by images of the self and its shadow ('Flowers in Darkness', 'The Place'), or of reflections in a mirror, as in 'Resurrection', or 'The Inner One', where she hints at the idea of a duality in one person. The idea of crossing over between one state and another is reinforced not only by contrasting images but also by her practice of transposing adjectives, as in 'A torrential tree in a leaf-drenched rain' ('Town Walk') or 'As if I'd never tasted corn/Had never seen a field of bread/Ripen...' ('Age').

Many of the poems, like the journals, start from a specific sight seen in narrow focus, then broaden and move away from the concrete as the writer meditates on the significance of what she has seen, concentrating almost impersonally on universal experiences not confined to a particular time or place. A few poems, however, reflect her response to a specific place. 'To the Mountains', for example, is inspired by living just on the English side of the Border, where the mountains to the west are at once familiar and mysterious. She has observed them in all their colours and seasons and feels 'my soul linked up/With the beginning and abiding of your light and world'. Yet she does not fully know them, for she 'cannot envisage/Them inhabited by people, cultivated, sown/With fields, orchards and cottages'. Nevertheless, in certain lights or moods 'I feel my spirit's path within my living feet', and she can achieve on a spiritual level a truer knowledge of those hills and her own relationship to them than if she had physically walked on them.

'The Harp' is also rooted in a particular place, for it was suggested by a house in Llangarron called Langstone Park where a 'dead harp' stood in the abandoned drawing room, described in a letter to Michael Williams (20 January 1944). This poem, evoking a house haunted by memories of a human tragedy, has an almost gothic mood, similar to that of the unfinished 'Widower's Tale' but it also owes something to the stories and bits of folklore which Margiad Evans used to pick up from Ellen Saunders, the woman in her sixties who lived next door to her at Potacre. She used to talk of 'floods, · love affairs, scandals, horses', entering fully into the spirit of each story, Margiad noted in her journal. 'I saw on her extraordinary face expressions of dead people who had been in their graves years when I was born ... I was looking at a living, looking, speaking model from memory' (21 September 1943). Margiad Evans often recounted these tales in letters to her husband and snippets soon began to find their way into her other writing. The reference in 'The Ballad of Mountain Vowr' to the boy calling 'Devil, do devil take bread and cheese', for example, is drawn directly from one of Ellen's recollections of her childhood (letter to Michael Williams, 14 March 1945). In this poem, which is in narrative form but without the usual, heavily accented ballad metre, Margiad Evans returns to the role of remembrancer of the forgotten and silenced which she had assumed in *Country Dance*. In the poem she tells the story of an unhappy, unloved man, whose very gravestone does not bear his name. His tale is told by a hedgecropper, who describes how the man's physical deformity came to be matched by a mind and behaviour equally unacceptable to the community. He was rejected, regarded as mad, and finally committed suicide, disfiguring himself further with his gun: 'at least he chose/The way he died'. In the classic authority formula of the traditional storyteller, the hedgecropper adds 'my grandfather's daddo was the man who held/The gate for the coffin cart to go through/Into the field', incidentally revealing how the forgotten, nameless man is kept alive in folk memory. The hedgecropper's realization of the life is as vivid as if he, and not his great-grandfather, had been the witness. With his further commemoration in the written poem, the dead man once again cheats time and death, triumphing too over those now-forgotten neighbours who drove him to suicide.

Such stories as these, and others based on more recent events, fed her prose writing as well as her poetry in the 1940s. Like poetry, the short story was a form well adapted to her circumstances, which did not allow long periods of sustained writing. From mid-1943 onwards her letters and journals refer increasingly often to working on stories. Occasionally these could be rattled off fairly quickly, but more often the process of drafting and rewriting was protracted. 'The Lost Fisherman', for example, seems to have been started in late 1943, judging by the comment, 'I *must* get poor Emily down to the river', in her journal that December, but the story was not finished to her satisfaction for another eighteen months and it was the autumn of 1945 before she felt ready to offer it to Gwyn Jones. By the following year, however, she had enough stories, some written, some only formed in her mind, for her to plan a book, and in February 1946 she signed a contract with the publisher Lindsay Drummond.

1947 started badly with a bitterly hard winter, with blizzards adding to the usual hardships. To make matters worse, in the spring their landlord gave them notice to leave Potacre as he wanted the cottage for one of his own workers who was getting married. Eventually Margiad and her husband acquired the tenancy of another cottage in Llangarron called Tower Hill, and were able to move in by the end of June. She had not been looking forward to the move, but the cottage improved on acquaintance, in spite of its over-grown garden which consumed time and energy to make productive. She began to feel more cheerful and settled back into her writing. Good news came in August when Robert Herring accepted for *Life and Letters* an essay entitled 'The Man with the Hammer'. It is a celebration of two musicians, the seventeenth-century violin maker, Jacob Stainer, and Jan Rosé, a paralysed Jewish émigré violinist whom Margiad had got to know while she lived at Llangarron and who had been her most inspiring music teacher.

September brought a visit from her French friend Nell, whom she had not seen for years. She regaled them with dreadful tales of her wartime experiences in occupied France, while helping to make the plum jam. Life was returning to normal. At the end of October Margiad and Mike celebrated their seventh wedding anniversary 'by opening a tin of milk unfit for babies and eating it with porridge by the fire' (diary, 28 October 1947). A fortnight later proofs arrived of her collection of short stories, *The Old and the Young*. 'Now the silence is broken' she declared (diary, 10 November 1947).

Over the last few years she had kept up her painting and draw-ing, and her new publisher, Lindsay Drummond, agreed to include illustrations by her in the book, and twelve of these were also incor-porated in the book-jacket design. The ink line-drawings placed at the beginning and end of each story were described on the title page as 'decorations by the author', so for the first time in her published work the author and artist had become one. She was dissatisfied with the drawings, feeling that they were too heavy and not what she had intended. The tailpieces are perhaps less successful than the decorated initials at the head of each story, but both capture the mood of the written text and form a bridge between the reader and the writer's own vivid realization of her characters.

The Old and the Young appeared at last in November 1948. It contains fifteen stories of which one, 'The Wicked Woman' had been written at the Lough Pool Inn and first published as early as 1933, but all the rest were written in the 1940s. The longest, 'The Lost Fisherman', originally intended as the title story of the collection, takes as its starting point events in May 1940, when Margiad's brother had just been taken prisoner of war and her eldest sister, Betty, came to Ross with her three children to escape the blitz in London, leaving her husband behind. The effect of the war on the small country town is graphically evoked with all its tension and chaos: the 'tanks and dismembered 'planes ... swerving down the narrow streets', delayed trains disgorging bewildered families of strangers, fears that the railway bridge carrying the line across the street within yards of 17 Brookend could be targeted, since it was used by ammunition trains travelling from Hereford. In the uncertainty and tension of 'this terrible spring', the main protagonist, Emily, comes across the fisherman and through this encounter is able to become again 'the real Emily' that she was before, by remembering her childhood, again based on the author's own memories of life at her aunt's farm. Later she talks with the fisherman as they row up the river in a time and place apart, between town and country, between daylight and night-time, and this conversation brings an implicit understanding between the two, deeper than the words they have spoken. But it also helps Emily to voice thoughts she had never put into words, to come to terms with inevitable change, and to grasp the present as a strategy for survival in the face of a frightening future.

Although 'The Lost Fisherman' draws on experiences from before the author's marriage, other stories in the collection were inspired by more recent events. Perhaps the most topical at the time of publication was 'The Ruin', with its sensitive treatment of the difficulties of readjustment to married life for a couple reunited after the husband is demobbed, a common experience in the late 1940s. Some stories can be traced to Margiad's life in Llangarron. 'The Old Woman and the Wind', for example, undoubtedly reflects her experience of living on a hill-top in a cottage often buffetted by gales. More specifically, 'The Boy who called for a light', in which the child, Derry, is notorious for knocking on people's doors and asking to borrow things, retells imaginatively how in November 1944 a little boy known to Margiad Evans called at Potacre and asked her to lend him a torch to find his way home. Relatives supplied other material: it was her mother-in-law's story of Bernard and Hilda Williams as children walking home the twelve miles from Gloucester to Mitcheldean after missing the last bus late at night, which inspired 'All through the night'. Margiad got on well with her mother-in-law, 'Ma Williams', who was as 'full of tales as Ellen. I can see what she tells' (journal, 2 November 1947). Stories she heard from neighbours were similarly reworked, as they had been in poems like 'The Ballad of Mountain Vowr'. The tale of 'Thomas Griffiths and Parson Cope', for example, where the madness of the master seems to be rubbing off on to his increasingly eccentric gardener, was based on just such an anecdote, as she told Gwyn Jones (30 March 1944), whilst Mr Amos of Langstone was the source of Mr Gregory and his 'visions' in 'The Boy who called for a light'. Even where an immediate source is not known, the setting and atmosphere, the way of life depicted and the outlook of the characters often seem to derive from her experience of living in that particular part of the Herefordshire countryside near Ross, whether in Llangarron or her earlier homes. The characters' dialect too is drawn directly from what she heard around her; she transcribed in her journals and her letters to her husband words or expressions which caught her ear, or even conversations, and much of this material found its way into the dialogue in her stories.

Her aunt's farm appears not only in 'The Lost Fisherman' but also in 'The Old and the Young', the story which gives the collection its title. Here a number of the details of life at the farm, Ell Hall, are drawn from memories of the year she and her sister spent at Benhall, as comparison with the factual reminiscences recorded in 'The Immortal Hospital' confirms. Moreover, the family in 'The Old and the Young' is composed, like the Whistler family, of three sisters and a younger brother, and the two middle sisters, representing Peggy and Nancy, are called Arabella and Esther as they are in the overtly autobiographical *The Wooden Doctor*. The relationship between these two again parallels that of the younger Whistler sisters:

> The two sisters loved each other profoundly in spite of there being three wide years between them and no likeness. It was as though before they had been born they had been twins in eternity.
> (*The Old and the Young*, 172)

The narrator identifies herself explicitly with the elder of the two: 'I was Arabella', and her later, adult experiences also closely resemble those of the author. As she thinks about Tilly, the old lady who was fond of the girls, and wonders when she had died, she remarks: 'Probably it happened when I was away from home on one of those miserable excursions into life which always ended (urgently) in a stampede for my own country' (p. 166). This seems to refer to the pattern of Margiad's own life in the 1930s. Just occasionally the mingling of childhood memories of a vanished past with adult experiences of the modern world brings a nostalgic tone:

> The village has changed. Nobody there has ever heard of Tilly and Mr and Mrs Spring. The bridge has been widened for war traffic, and ruined, the eighteenth-century sundial has been carted away and left in a corner, a tomb without a grave.
> (*The Old and the Young*, 165)

But enough remains to help bring to life the memories which celebrate Tilly's life. Just as Tilly herself in her old age sees again her young self on the same spot, long after the old woman's death the sight of Tilly's house revives for the narrator both Tilly and her own self as a child, brought together in the image of Tilly once, unexpectedly, dancing in front of the children at Ell Farm. Tilly lives on after death as part of the narrator's remembered childhood.

The permanence of such memories of childhood is a recurring theme. 'The Boy who called for a light' may have been inspired by a recent incident in the writer's life, but the story is pushed back into the past and retold by the child become man, his boyhood evoked by concrete examples within a general meditation on memory:

> Our mothers cobbled and wrangled over the wounds in our faded clothing; our fathers patched our boots and swore. Well, that was the way home, and the queer thing is that after the first, the first one you remember, there's never another, not even when you're a man, married, with your own children, living somewhere and going to work yourself. That one way you ran with your brothers and sisters and your child mates goes through your life, right back to the beginning, to the overcrowded table and the pink glass sugar bowl. It remains, a contrast to all others; like the old china when you go to buy crockery. You always see those first smudged garlands, those saucers, that thick cloam infant's plate that went down the family and ended as the cat's.
>
> (*The Old and the Young*, 62)

In exploring the nature and uses of memory, the stories often include a specific incident which unlocks the door to a clearly visualized past with the sudden power of Proust's madeleine dipped in lime-flower tea, a past to which the rememberer is transported before being returned with as intense a shock to the present. Listening in her mother's house to the canaries in their cage 'cracking their seeds with a tiny insect-like pop', Emily in 'The Lost Fisherman' is momentarily back in the country:

> It was so hot that the stones were tepid in the shade. The pods of broom and gorse burnt in the sun with that wee minute crack, with only the linnet to make the stillness alive. Emily remembered as if she saw the burnt grass and the sky above, the clicking and whirring world of heat.
>
> (*The Old and the Young*, 92)

This process is the starting point and main theme of 'Miss Potts and Music', where the narrator, attempting to write an article, gazes out of the window and seems to glimpse a child swinging in the branches of a tree, a child who unexpectedly brings back the thought of her old music teacher's niece. Here too, as in 'The Old and the Young', there is an unfinished, enigmatic element, for the stories of these remembered people are unfinished: the narrator does not know when Tilly died or what became of Miss Potts after her family went to live in Weymouth. Their lives touched only at one time and place, and at best only vivid but brief glimpses of them can be conjured from memory.

The remembered past is incomplete but not idealized. The life of many of the characters has been hard and they may have experienced unhappiness or disappointment. Emily's mother in 'The Lost Fisherman' wanted to be a professional musician but her father would not allow it, and Emily imagines her 'leaving her joy behind forever and then all the troubles and the hard work and the poverty falling on her'. Her only gain was four children: 'a poor substitute for Bach' (p. 100). In 'A Modest Adornment' Miss Plant in her youth had walked to London because she could not bear to live apart from the woman she loved, but lived thereafter starved of signs of affection until she is on her death-bed, and even then it is not her companion but a neighbour who comforts her. The lack of communication and true understanding between two people, such as Miss Plant and Miss Allensmoore, is a theme touched on elsewhere. In both 'Into Kings' and 'Solomon' a mother suddenly finds herself distanced from her son, unable to comprehend what he thinks and sees. Just as those mothers for a moment perceive their sons as strangers, so too in 'The Ruin', the wife is suddenly made aware of a new distance between herself and her much-loved husband, newly returned from the war. In this case the distance has been caused by his absence, for he has seen and experienced things that she has not shared, and now 'sees' the dilapidated cottage and its potential with very different eyes from hers, whereas once their vision would have been the same. There is always a gap between hope, expectation or illusion on the one hand and reality on the other.

Small mercies bring comfort to these stories, however, as darkness is unexpectedly transformed into light, even if only temporarily. In 'Into Kings', for example, the sudden revelation of beauty glimpsed by the little boy not only transfigures the poor family's cottage but also leads to a new sympathy between himself and the invalid daughter, crippled in body and mind. Miss Plant's last days are warmed by the kindness of Mrs Webb and the green gloves she knitted for her, even if they come almost too late. Blessings may be mixed but they are still welcome: thus the exhausted Mrs Pike in 'Mrs Pike's Eldorado' is able to leave her second husband who treats her like a slave because she knows that with her sister the hard work will be softened by sharing and by love. Similarly Mrs Ashstone in 'The Old Woman and the Wind', discovering that the grass is not in fact greener on the other side, learns to live with the familiar disadvantages of her hill-top cottage and even to gain comfort from them. Life is not perfect, but a compromise makes it bearable.

Although there are male characters in these stories, Margiad Evans returns repeatedly to the domestic world of rural women and their children, and as the book's title suggests, it is with the very youngest and very oldest that she has most sympathy. What she presented in *Autobiography* of the child's way of seeing gives her in these stories the rare ability to see the world through a child's eyes. Here again is the closeness of focus, the acceptance of the incomprehensible, the investing of the ordinary with mysterious meaning, especially in 'Solomon' and 'Into Kings'. The freedom of the young child is parallelled in the very old who are their nearest allies, and between them there can be moments of sudden intimacy, as Derry experiences with Kate in 'The Boy who called for a light'. Love between the old and the young is unconditional, as in 'The Lost Fisherman', where Emily's mother's love 'for her own children was all anxiety, only what she felt for grandchildren was physical and enjoyable', and the young mothers in these stories are often distant, rather detached from the children, sometimes barely sketched in. Here, however, there seems to be a class distinction, for the relationships of working-class mothers with their children are shown as warmer and more straightforward than in families higher up the social scale.

In general the working women are the most vivid creations in *The Old and the Young*. In the absence of any cenotaph for them, Margiad Evans honours their labour in these stories as she had in 'The Passionate Refusal'. The villages, perhaps reflecting those of the writer's childhood during and immediately after the First World War, are populated mainly by women, their men often dead, weak or elderly, or simply off-stage. 'A Modest Adornment' shows the beginning of a typical day's work for the women: 'cracking wood, carrying pigswill and paddling out to feed the poultry', or making a seven o'clock pudding (which must boil from seven until noon). Work continues to the day's end for women like Kate Owen, scrubbing her floor after dark in 'The Boy who called for a light'. Those living outside the village bear additional burdens. Like Margiad Evans herself at Potacre, Mrs Ashstone in 'The Old Woman and the Wind' not only has to contend with the gales but also drag her shopping home uphill:

> Later on she trod her way upwards with her groceries and a bucket of shallots Mary Maddocks had run out to give her. They were very heavy, but she stopped to gather a handful of bracken, bending the canes over and over to fit her small grate. The climb made her tremble. The wind took her breath and threw it away as if it were nothing. 'There's no mercy, no mercy', she began to whimper, feeling her hair blowing awry, and her knees clutched invisibly.
> (*The Old and the Young*, 31-2)

In her fictional portrayal of the harsh realities of life for countrywomen like these, Margiad Evans has close affinities with her older contemporary, the Welsh-language writer, Kate Roberts (1891-1985). Both writers in their short stories depict a domestic world in a rural or semi-rural community where the women's lives are full of hardship and struggle. Although there is bleakness at times, there is above all bravery and dignity in these women. In their depiction of children too, Margiad Evans and Kate Roberts show warmth, humour and great insight, and it is interesting to note that when *The Old and the Young* was published Margiad Evans, like Kate Roberts, was childless. Without children of their own to observe, both women seem to have drawn on memories of their own childhood, and these come to form one of the most important sources of inspiration and material for their writing. Despite their very different origins and circumstances, there is considerable affinity in their stories and in fact they deeply admired each other's work.

Although they never met, Kate Roberts and Margiad Evans corresponded between 1946 and 1952. Contact between them started after Robert Herring commissioned Margiad to review *A Summer's Day*, a collection of Kate Roberts's stories in English translation.

FLOWERS UNDER FALLEN LEAVES

When Kate Roberts read the review in *Life and Letters To-day* in November 1946 she immediately wrote to thank her. 'Others', she noted, 'have praised without understanding'. Only Margiad had seen the universality of her work and put the setting of the stories into their true context. Margiad Evans had laid particular emphasis on the 'universal spirit' of Kate Roberts's stories; set as they are in the Caernarfonshire quarrying districts they are 'as narrow in scene as they are wide in inference', a point which Kate took up in her letter:

> I am so glad you have spoken about the universal theme for tragedy in the stories ... I cannot see why an author who can take any country for his background has any more to say about life than an author who has stayed at home. To my mind the latter has all the advantages. I think that richness of expression comes from the depth of one's knowledge of one small part of this earth, it does not matter whether that be a pool of tadpoles or the Court of Louis XIV.
> (12 November 1946)

Margiad Evans's sympathetic appreciation stemmed partly from her familiarity with the area in which the stories are set, thanks to her stay at Pontllyfni in 1932. She recalls in her review how she could see Snowdon from her window there, and uses the image of 'the small window containing the mountain' as a metaphor for the *multum in parvo* of Kate Roberts's work. They had much in common, moreover, as women writers living outside a metropolitan centre. Both were in danger of being marginalized by English critics, especially since they chose to write about what they knew best, rather than what might be acceptable or fashionable. Despite the difference of age, language and background, both shared the same concerns in their writing at this time, and this is what gave Margiad such insight into Kate Roberts's work. Indeed some of her most perceptive comments in the review of Kate Roberts's work, such as the universality of human experience within a circumscribed setting, are equally applicable to her own. Similarly she also refers to 'a deceptive quietness which draws upon the intuition of the reader for its final effect', a comment perhaps even truer of Margiad Evans's stories, which require the reader to reflect before the significance of what has happened in the narrative can be fully grasped.

The affinities in their work raise the question of influence in one direction or the other, especially as by 1946 they were familiar with each other's work. Kate Roberts recalled reading *The Wooden Doctor* and some of Margiad Evans's short stories, probably the three which appeared in *The Welsh Review* between 1939 and 1946, namely 'The Black House', 'All through the night' and 'The Lost Fisherman'. Although Margiad was restricted to such examples of Kate Roberts's work as had appeared in English, she was a regular reader of *The Welsh Review* and *Life and Letters To-day*, where a number of these translations had been published since 1939. She had much admired them and had congratulated Gwyn Jones on publishing 'Old Age' by Kate Roberts (30 March 1944). Since Kate Roberts was working within the Welsh-language tradition and had already chosen her literary path before coming into contact with Margiad Evans's short stories, it seems highly unlikely that she had been influenced by the younger woman.

It is striking, however, how often the two women choose similar themes for their stories: the relationship between two elderly sisters ('Chwiorydd' and 'Mrs Pike's Eldorado'), for example, or a sensitive portrayal of an intimate, perhaps lesbian, relationship between two women ('Nadolig', 'Y Trysor' and 'A Modest Adornment'). Themes common to both authors are set against a similar background of the hard lives of women. An essential ingredient they also share is the acceptance and understanding of the fact that love between two people can take very many shapes and forms, and both writers lack any romantic, sentimental or idealized concept of marriage or love. In portraying a marriage or similar relationship, both Margiad and Kate are concerned at times with lack of communication and understanding between the partners. As we have seen, Margiad Evans explored this theme in 'The Ruin', one of the stories included in *The Old and the Young*, where the treatment of this theme is strikingly similar to that in 'Y Golled' by Kate Roberts, which appears in *A Summer's Day*. In both cases the story unfolds through the eyes of the wife and in both the couple seem at the start to be happy and united as they enjoy a day out together. When tensions and especially distances begin to appear between them during the outing, it is the wife who is most aware of this and tries to bridge the gap.

Kate Roberts notes that the wife 'knew exactly how he felt, but of her thoughts he was unaware', whilst Margiad's Jessy asks herself whether 'her flashes of communication' ever reach her husband's mind. Both writers make subtle use of dialogue as well as authorial comment to suggest the increasing distance of the husband from his wife. It is just possible that in this instance Margiad Evans had been directly influenced by Kate Roberts's story. She must have read the English version of 'Y Golled' at the end of June or beginning of July 1946, for she was writing her review of *A Summer's Day* for *Life and Letters* in early July that year. 'The Ruin' was published in *Life and Letters* in January 1947 and so must have been submitted to the editor by the autumn or early winter, but the exact date of composition has not been found in her surviving journals.

Even if the similarities between these two stories were no more than coincidental, the numerous affinities between the stories of Kate Roberts and Margiad Evans in general suggest that they had developed similar techniques, concerns and outlook independently of each other, largely through the experiences they had in common as women, especially their familiarity with the harsh realities of life for women in the communities where they had spent their formative years. Their intimate knowledge of life in those communities, in its domestic detail and the influence of the changing seasons and weather, and their confidence in writing out of and about those experiences set them apart from so many of their contemporaries. Both were indifferent to the pull of the metropolis and to literary fashion: 'Oh crikey, I cry', exclaimed Margiad Evans to Gwyn Jones in January 1947, 'why must poets be so *sophisticated* today?' Instead both Margiad Evans and Kate Roberts concentrated on listening to the compulsive voice inside that drove them to write and to give expression to what that voice spoke to them. Both ploughed lonely furrows, but their correspondence reveals their support for each other. Questions of language, nationality or status did not obtrude as through their letters they offered each other not only comfort in solitude, pain or illness, but above all encouragement, support, love and understanding of each other as women writers.

Seven
A Ray of Darkness (1949-1952)

The publication of *The Old and the Young* did not mark the end of short-story writing for Margiad Evans. It is true that at times she felt constricted by the form: 'When I'm trying to write short stories my hand feels as if it were in a tight glove', she had noted in her journal in January 1944, but she continued to write further stories in the late 1940s and early 1950s. In April 1948 she heard the nightingale singing in Llangarron and from that incident sprang 'A Party for the Nightingale', which was immediately accepted by Gwyn Jones and published in *The Welsh Review* the following winter. In this story a child and four adults are subtly presented as locked in their own separate worlds with little genuine communication between them, recalling some of the tales in *The Old and the Young*. One of the characters, Miss Boyce, who goes off alone and hears the nightingale, has affinities with the narrator of *Autobiography*. The manuscript included an ink drawing in the same style as those in *The Old and the Young*, but this did not appear with the story in *The Welsh Review*. For Margiad Evans, however, it was still important to provide her own visual commentary on the written text. That she planned to include illustrations in a second volume of short stories is shown by a note, dated 28 January 1948, inside the manuscript of an unpublished story, 'Pereena'. Addressed to the publisher Lindsay Drummond, the note explains that 'Pereena' belonged to 'a collection of uneasy stories which I call The Blessing of the Trumpets ... I want to draw for them all'. Some drawings were in fact made, for the manuscript of one story, 'The Master Died', written in 1947, includes five ink drawings. By late August 1948 Margiad Evans had planned the proposed new volume and listed its contents in her journal. This collection, which never materialised, was to include twelve stories. Some of these were finished but some existed only in her mind. Six, including 'A Party for the Nightingale', 'Pereena' and 'The Master Died', can be identified with extant manuscript texts from their present titles. Although some of these tales focus on relationships between people, at least two are concerned with the supernatural, and 'The Master Died' shares much of the atmosphere of the unfinished 'Widower's Tale'.

Apart from poems and stories, Margiad Evans was writing and publishing a few essays. In the first of these, 'Three Seas', which appeared in *Life and Letters To-day* in 1945, she combined past and present in a new way, bringing together material from her recent wartime journals with passages from the record she had kept of her visit to Iceland with Ruth Farr in 1936. Ruth came to stay with her at Potacre in 1942, and this may have revived memories and caused Margiad to reread her notes. In the essay, impressions of sea and harbour in Iceland are juxtaposed with passages from her journals recording her visits to her husband at two naval bases, first in 1943 and finally in 1944, their last meeting before he was posted abroad. But she also evokes an even earlier period in her life, for seeing a Breton sailor at Dartmouth suddenly brings back her stay in Pouldu in her late teens. Here, as in *The Old and the Young*, something observed in the present transports her to an earlier time, which is clearly visualized:

> Crowds of sailors here in D-, but I've seen no other face like this sea peasant's, compressed of numbers I'd known. His face was a *place* to me – Bas Pouldu. I saw the wall, the salmon nets, the river, and the chestnut trees in the meadow where Henri Poulin and Rodney and I went gathering ... and all the others – Léonie, Finette the sad, Mélanie in her different coif...

Just as in *Autobiography* Nature with its repeated cycles was seen as ever changing yet always the same, so too in this essay the sea in Brittany, Iceland and England is both different and the same, the 'Three Seas' are all one, and unite her memories of different periods in her life. The sea even recalls her inland home at Llangarron, for its sound reminds her of the rustling wheatfield around the cottage. However, 'Three Seas' is very much a response to contemporary events, for the war and her imminent parting from her husband lie heavily on it: 'the war presses into my heart *always*; and in M– the whole terror focuses'.

'Arcadians and Barbarians', an essay on English traditional song, published in 1949 in *Life and Letters To-day*, returns to a theme in her earlier essay, 'The Man with the Hammer', for it is concerned with music and the way it bridges time. Just as in that earlier essay the violin formed a link between the instrument maker and Margiad's own violin teacher, so too in 'Arcadians and Barbarians' English songs link the past period of their making with the present moment of performance. 'Byron and Emily Brontë' likewise touches on long-standing concerns, for both these writers had been of consuming interest to her since at least her early twenties, and had left their mark on her novels, as we have seen. By the beginning of 1944 she was meditating on an essay on their affinities, but it was the end of September 1947 before she managed to start writing the first draft. She sent it to Gwyn Jones for his opinion and rewrote parts of it in response to his criticisms before it was published in June 1948 in *Life and Letters To-day*, with a prefatory letter to him.

Although on the surface the essay is a comparative study of Byron and Emily Brontë as writers and individuals, it is also a highly personal piece of writing, the result of so many years' meditation on the subject. Much of what she says about them can also be seen with hindsight as an analysis of her own life. She argues that although there were fundamental differences between the two, both writers had in common a particular poetic voice and diction, the same 'energetic expression of lonely passion' seen 'in no two other poets in English', and particularly evident in *Manfred* and *Wuthering Heights*. In each of those works the main character possesses 'the same capacity for investing fury with tragedy, mere rage with an inner ecstasy of woe'. But she moves far beyond literary criticism in her main thesis, which was what Gwyn Jones found difficult. She argues that both Emily Brontë and Byron were mystics, defining a mystic for her present purposes as 'one who consciously holds sustained relations with the absolute', a quality she found also in composers like Mozart and Beethoven and writers such as George Herbert, Blake, Thoreau and Melville. Furthermore, she believes that for such a mystic, life becomes above all a preparation for death, for 'the ultimate state of mysticism can be described as pacifism towards death'. In other words, when the mystic achieves his or her full revelation, there can be nothing left but death. 'When the spirit reaches finality the body can't go on living', because 'the active principle' which guards life in the body has left. This, above all else, is what makes these two writers 'twin poets', for 'in the manner of their dying, as in their poetry, Byron and Emily Brontë show their likeness to each other. Neither climate nor consumption was responsible for their deaths, but detachment. Nothing could have saved them or altered the fact'. By their different paths they had reached the same understanding.

This idea of death as the climax of life recalls her own *Autobiography* where death is accepted as a part of the oneness of life. She accepted Derek Savage's idea that a 'death wish' was present in her work, but felt he had misunderstood its nature. 'To long for death may be to long for resurrection. It was penetrating of you to discern the wish: you do not understand that one may wish to be stronger through death' (24 March 1950). Her attitude towards death was a positive one, without any morbidness or even sadness, because for her death is above all a life-enhancing concept, an idea often found in her journals. 'A lonely person lives already in Eternity', she wrote in May 1944. 'The only story of death is a life story', adding: 'Not that I mean to write mine.' In her journals for 1947 and 1948 such references to her early death proliferate. 'To write the story of one's life from the end would be a ghost story,' she wrote in February 1948. 'I can tell the time will come when I shall be numb and unable to choose or even know a word. What is it, this numbness, confusion, forgetfulness? Is it mental or physical?' Today those words, read in knowledge of what was to follow, seem curiously prophetic, for in *A Ray of Darkness*, her next book after *The Old and the Young*, she would begin to write the story of her death. Although she was unaware of it at the time, the illness that would eventually kill her was already at work, the illness whose onset and first two years of development are chronicled and analysed in *A Ray of Darkness*.

The two years before the first clear sign of what would be diag-nosed as epilepsy were again unsettled. In July 1948, just a year after she and her husband had left Potacre for Tower Hill, they heard that the farm where Michael Williams worked had been sold. At the beginning of December they were given notice to quit the cottage, and Michael Williams lost his job. By the end of January they were homeless. Margiad's distress is evident from a letter she wrote to her friend Margaret Scudamore that February: 'I'm in the most terrible muddle I find. My clothes are here and there and money is a terrible problem with none coming in ... I get in a panic'. For Margiad this period was traumatic. She had to leave Llangarron which had been her home for seven years, and that part of Herefordshire which she loved so deeply. 'I was desolated and nearly dead of separation', she recalled in a letter to Derek Savage in April 1950. 'You may say Nature is nature everywhere, but it wasn't so to Emily Brontë, nor to me. Language is language everywhere, but not native language.' To Bryher she confided her hope that she would 'never feel the same passion for a countryside again' (10 September 1949), as she could not face experiencing a second time such pain of separation. The grief of exile was to be aggravated by being away from her husband. Michael Williams had decided to train as a teacher and, after some months of short-term work, that autumn he started a course at St Paul's College, Cheltenham.

When she left Llangarron at the end of January Margiad had gone to stay in Buckinghamshire with her sister Nancy, who had recently moved to Chalfont St Peter. Here, in the area where she had lived as a small child before moving to Herefordshire, and in the very house where her mother had been brought up, Margiad found comfort. 'In those smaller fields and woods this spring I found the spirit of all I'd loved so dearly elsewhere faithful and unchanged ... and it literally saved me', she told Bryher (1 November 1949). It was here, on 15 April 1949, that she received a letter out of the blue from the writer John Lehmann. On behalf of the Society of Authors, he offered her £125 through their travelling fund provided by an anonymous donor. 'I felt my face go deep red with shock', she noted in her journal. To have been selected for the award that year gave Margiad a much-needed boost. It also gave her the chance to take her first real holiday with her husband, for the only other occasions when they had spent time together away from home had been her brief visits to him when he was in the Navy, and those had been overshadowed with anxiety.

The only conditions of the award were that the money must be spent on travel before the end of the year, and outside Britain. Margiad would have loved to go to New England, home of Thoreau, but that was beyond their means, and continental Europe did not appeal, so they decided to go to Ireland. As they set out Margiad thought gleefully of all the meals she would not have to cook during the next three weeks. They travelled by train to Fishguard where they met many of Michael's relations before sailing on 11 August to Waterford. Once on board, they found that the ship's master was Captain Mendus, one of Michael's distant cousins, who took them onto the bridge and invited them to spend the night in the chart house instead of below with the other passengers. From Waterford they travelled to Kerry and then on to Dublin, where they saw the sights and had a very social time. They were introduced to a host of interesting people and Margiad was recorded reading three of her unpublished poems. It was with regret that they made their way back to Waterford and rejoined Captain Mendus on board the ferry on 4 September.

The journal of that holiday, illustrated with many sketches, she kept not for herself but for her as yet anonymous benefactor. Apart from this journal, the visit to Ireland seems to have left few traces in Margiad's literary work, but it was valuable in other ways. Even allowing that it was written for the benefactor, the journal shows clearly how much the visit meant to her after the wartime years of toil and stress. From the urban charms of Dublin to the quiet and calm of the unspoilt countryside, Ireland with all its eccentricities delighted and soothed her. Apart from an acute attack of her old enemy, cystitis, which kept her to her bed for a couple of days, she felt strong and well. It was 'a time of bliss'.

The benefactor soon disclosed that she was the American writer Winifred Ellerman, better known as Bryher, then living in Switzerland. Bryher, who used her wealth to support and encourage less fortunate writers, continued to send presents of money and of practical items such as food in the years that followed. She was so generous that Margiad Evans felt almost guilty and often urged her not to give her any more. But even more important than this material help was the supportive friendship of one woman writer to another which Bryher offered her. They corresponded regularly from the moment when Margiad first wrote in September 1949 to thank her for the holiday and to send her the journal she had kept. The letters document not only the practicalities of her life but also her ideas and aspirations, and despite the fact that she was never again to enjoy the health and energy last experienced in Ireland, they contain no self-pity or bitterness.

Margiad still had no home of her own, and from September, when Michael Williams started at college, she lived in Gloucester with her sister-in-law Hilda, at the top of a house in St Aldate's Street. From the windows a roofscape stretched before her, which inspired her to pick up her drawing again. During the day it was hard to get down to writing so she would wait until the night, when she worked with 'a sort of concentrated will'. Although she still did not feel able to finish the languishing 'Widower's Tale', nor to start the full-length study on Emily Brontë which was increasingly on her mind, that autumn she did finish a short story, 'A Gentleman from Jerusalem' and an essay on child development and children in literature, both begun the previous year and both left unpublished at her death.

After much fruitless searching, towards the end of September the couple heard of a cottage that might suit them. It was at Elkstone, a village about six miles south of Cheltenham, where Michael Williams was studying, and it stood high up on a hill at a thousand feet above sea level. It was called the Black House, for its walls outside had been painted with tar. They had to wait for the existing tenant, a very grubby old woman, to move out, and for the landlord to arrange for some repairs and for the house to be scrubbed clean, but by the end of March 1950 they were able to move in. The disadvantages were no drains, no running water and a long way to the bus and the shops, but the rent was only £23 a year and it was just Margiad's kind of house:

> Some minute muslin curtains were made for the windows, the

geraniums were set in them, the old black flagstones were polished, the coppers shone in the log-light of the open kitchen fire. The whole of the inside was painted a clear yellow, including the charming little old staircase.

It had a parlour like a nut. There were four rooms, an outdoor lavatory, a lean-to wash-house with an earth floor, and a pigscot. At the gateway stood an immensely tall pine. All its branches went up in the air except one, which it held stiffly over the roof, in a commanding gesture.

(*A Ray of Darkness*, 69)

She was sure she would be able to write here, and was keen to settle down to writing the book on Emily Brontë which she had been meditating for so long. This time, she declared, she would not make of housekeeping and gardening a rod for her own back. 'Once I couldn't have left a greasy sink or an unwiped gas stove', she confessed to Bryher, 'but my hands are tired of damp rags' (2 January 1950). 'My cottage won't shine this time, but let's hope it will be filled with manuscripts.' She was to be on her own for much of the time, because in term time Michael Williams stayed at the college in Cheltenham from Monday to Friday and came home only at weekends. But she found her neighbours kind and welcoming, and soon made friends with the couple at the next house along the lane. And she liked Elkstone itself, with its ancient church, rich in curious carved stone decoration. The countryside was 'splendid, most beautiful, most wild and in parts anxiously *violent*' she told Bryher (4 April 1950). It was full of wild flowers and, as the village was so high up, often in the clouds, the air was never still: 'on the hottest day ... you could feel a little frill of breeze under your chin like a beard, and your hair alive' (*A Ray of Darkness*, 69). 'I was only to live there one year, but never to gain so much of the intangibleness of a place as I did there' (p. 62). It was a 'hard, rough, tiring life', but although there were moments of miserable exhaustion, when the spring arrived, a month later than in the town far below, the garden was planted and she could relax a little. It was on 11 May that, alone in the Black House, she suffered her first major fit.

In fact, as she later realized, she had had slight warning signs for years, since childhood. She describes them in *A Ray of Darkness* as 'moments of separation from my consciousness – moments when I was quite literally conscious and unconscious at the same time ... I have often crossed a room, and while not losing sight or bearings, not known how I crossed it' (pp. 38-9). Unaware of the implications of these symptoms, she had also described such an experience in *Turf or Stone*. In the novel Mary, the unwilling wife of Easter Probert, describes the sensation to the master:

> 'Something like a telephone rings in my head, and then my neck seems to go numb, and though I always go on with what I'm doing, I haven't an idea what it is ... I have walked quite a long way and come to myself and wondered how I did it, for I couldn't remember a thing.'
> She rubbed the back of her neck gently:
> 'When I was a child I thought the ringing was meant for a warning, and I used to say out loud, "Thank you, thank you ... message received."'
> (*Turf or Stone*, 124)

Rereading her journals whilst writing *A Ray of Darkness* in 1951, she noticed that these spells had come more frequently from 1948 onwards and were perhaps connected with the feeling of being tired and rushed. An entry in February 1948 refers to 'rays of oblivion' around her, a phrase which may have inspired the book's title, although 'rays of darkness' occurs in a very different context in her poem 'How things seem' (*Poems from Obscurity*, 31).

On the night of her first fit she had been sitting writing in the parlour and at about eleven o'clock got up to make some tea. When consciousness returned to her it was twenty-five past midnight. At first she thought she had fallen asleep but as her mind cleared she realized that this was not the case, for she had fallen between the fender before the open fire and the table where her oil lamp still stood burning:

> The space in which I was lying was perhaps a yard wide. My sleeve was charred by an ember, but this was all. Had some special agent of preservation laid me down between lamp and fire it could not have been more dexterously done ... My head was turned so that my opening eyes could not do otherwise than see the clock face. After a fit, the one unforgettable sight is the first thing one sees consciously. And this little green enamel alarm

clock, our only time-piece, given to us years before for a wedding present, whose heart had ticked through so many solitary
nights and evenings all through the war, became at once more
than it had ever been, a memory and a reality. It frightened me
for a moment, but only as the face of a friend who tells incomprehensible news. I simply stared at it. [...]
   I must have turned my head, for the next things I saw were
my dog's beautiful yellow eyes. They were fixed on me and she
was lying in her basket.
   (*A Ray of Darkness*, 79-80)

She had 'fallen through Time, Continuity and Being'. At first she
could not grasp what had happened, for 'the brain held and let go,
held and let go, a confused mass of atmosphere and memory. It
worked, but like an engine misfiring and unsteered' (p. 80).
Gradually she focused on another image, still as yet unstable, which
was her blue-banded quart milk-jug, and she remembered that she
had not poured into it the can of milk fetched from the farm that
afternoon. Feeling sick, she opened the door and went out into the
fresh air and then became aware that her clothes were damp. It was
this sign of incontinence that made her realize that she had had a fit.
Looking again at the room where she fell, she saw that her cup had
been knocked over, spilling tea on her manuscript. She tidied up,
washed and changed, then walked in a daze up the road with her
dog to wake up her neighbours. They calmly put her to bed in their
house and telephoned the college to summon her husband. The next
day the local doctor called to see her at the Black House and decided
she should see a specialist, Professor Frederick Golla at the Burden
Neurological Institute near Bristol. She had already had some contact with epileptics, for there was a colony for sufferers of the disorder near her sister's house at Chalfont St Peter; Margiad was used
to seeing the residents and remembered that her mother used to go
to play the piano for them. But in the month she had to wait before
her appointment she was overcome with anxiety about the implications of the diagnosis that seemed to her only too certain.
   She tried to lead as normal a life as possible, and ten days after
the fit even started to write her book on Emily Brontë, not just as a
distraction but because she hoped 'that through the darkness I
might see her more clearly'. But it proved impossible. In her present

state of mind, Margiad Evans felt ideas streaming in upon her uncontrollably and could not focus on the one woman she was trying to understand and interpret, although she did find poems coming to her, sudden and urgent. But she was still in a state of shock and fear which prevented clear, detached thought. It was a relief when the day came to travel to Bristol for her appointment.

At their very first meeting she took to Professor Golla, that 'great detective of neurotic diseases'. He was one of the most experienced specialists in the field, then in his early seventies, and had been director of the Burden Neurological Institute since 1939. The correspondence that subsequently passed between him and Margiad Evans, as well as references in her letters to others, shows how much she trusted and admired him. He too developed a great respect and affection for her, finding her interesting as a person as well as a patient. After establishing a picture of what had happened, he decided that she had indeed suffered an epileptic fit and that her condition had its origins in a riding accident in her childhood. At the age of nine she had fallen off a horse, hitting the back of her head, and he thought that the slight scarring in the brain that this had caused was the reason for the fits. Drugs were prescribed to control the symptoms and Margiad was urged to live as normal a life as possible. But although she had no further fits for three months, her life had changed utterly. After this turning point, finding herself now on 'the other side of the wave', she not only found her old interest in the idea of death returning, but became convinced that she would not live for many more years, even though she knew that people did not die of fits.

But coming to terms with her new identity as an epileptic was not the only major change in her life which she had to face. In late July 1950, when she and her husband went back to Chalfont St Peter for a holiday with her sister Nancy and her family, Margiad found herself increasingly exhausted. She could only assume that she was either very ill or pregnant, and presently discovered that she was in fact pregnant. She was then forty-one 'and had assuredly never expected motherhood'. It must have been a tremendous shock, although she argues in *A Ray of Darkness* that as a writer she was perhaps better prepared than other women for this new state: 'To create, although in another form, something from within me, was a commonplace'. Nonetheless, she was aware of the potential conflict between physical creativity and the intellectual or artistic creativity which she considered the most impelling:

> Triumph I did feel, inseparable from the fulfilment of the purpose for which I was a woman: but I confess that it was a lesser one than I had already had in finding a child in the womb of my brain. Humanly it may be the supreme outlet for a woman's passion – to bear a child; but artistically it is not; and I will never agree that it can lastingly influence a woman artist away from her greatest instinct. The neglect of many children by intellectual mothers may be due to this – that the brain and the womb are enemy cities, and the inhabitants of them are born to strive with one another.
>
> (*A Ray of Darkness*, 120-1)

But if the realization that she was to have a child 'brought less shock of pleasure than achievement in other ways' it did bring a sense of responsibility absent in the creation of a work of art. Initially her pregnancy made creative work seem unlikely but brought much-needed calm and relaxation. In August she was pleased to be invited to submit part of the manuscript of *Autobiography* for an exhibition in London that the National Book League were organizing as part of the Festival of Britain celebrations the following year. But at the end of that month, back home in the Black House, she had another fit. Now 'the light ... held patches of invisible darkness,' she noted, and time had become a rotten, worm-eaten floor, treacherous and unreliable beneath her feet. It was this second bad fit that made her wonder whether it was right to continue the pregnancy. Although abortion was then illegal, this solution was suggested to her, and, in her terror that she might pass the epilepsy on to her child, for a while she asked herself whether it should not be born. But both her local doctor and Professor Golla reassured her. Since her fits derived from physical damage, not from a hereditary condition, there was no danger of her passing it on. She wept two tears: 'One it seemed was mine, and one the child's' (*A Ray of Darkness*, 129).

But she could no longer live alone, in case of any accident if she had further fits during pregnancy, and so arrangements were made for her to have someone with her during the week while her husband was in Cheltenham. This help was paid for by Bryher, who had taken a personal interest in Margiad's situation and was keen to offer assistance. The pregnancy proceeded fairly normally and on 22 March 1951 Margiad Evans gave birth to Cassandra Ellen Williams at the maternity home in Cheltenham. The doctors had hoped that after the physical changes of childbirth she would be less prone to fits, but eight days after the birth she suffered another fit and thereafter could no longer breastfeed. There could be no question now of living in the Black House, alone with her baby, under the constant threat of fits, so the family moved into a house in Leckhampton Road, Cheltenham. In May Margiad Evans was granted £225 by the Royal Literary Fund for the safe upbringing of her daughter, allowing her to pay for someone to attend her for most of the day while her husband was out.

The fear of fits that was now always at the back of her mind was made worse not only by her new responsibility to her child, but also by one of the effects of taking drugs to control the fits. Whereas before she had been mercifully unaware of the approach of a fit, because oblivion hit her before any realization of what was happening, she now suffered a few dreadful moments at the onset, when she knew that she was about to have a fit but could do nothing about it, and the fits left her with a sense of terrible grief. This sadness when consciousness returned she could only account for by the idea that her 'soul had been somewhere or seen some one who was Peace and completion, and that it had left that presence to come back to me' (*A Ray of Darkness*, 149). Small wonder that she felt an understanding of the 'wonderful serene longing for death' which Albert Schweitzer had discerned in the music of Bach. Her poem 'Gemini', composed in October 1951, would seem on first reading to be inspired by the twin-like relationship between a mother and her child, but in *A Ray of Darkness* she explains that it was addressed 'both to my child and to death, separately, or together' (p. 145).

The name she had chosen for her child also reflects her feelings in the early months of her pregnancy. During the summer of 1948 she had felt that her poetic thinking had been dominated by the image of Apollo, god of light, medicine, wisdom and music. He appears not only in poems but in the short story, 'A Party for the Nightingale' where his image comes to Miss Boyce when she distances herself from the rest of the party. But in the summer of 1950 another figure had moved into the foreground, that of Cassandra, 'seer and virgin, beloved of Apollo' (*A Ray of Darkness*, 112), after whom she named her daughter. What Margiad Evans does not mention is that Cassandra's chief role in the tale of Troy is that of a prophetess doomed never to be believed. This inevitably brings to mind Margiad's prediction that she would not live into old age, which her friends had refused to take seriously.

After the upheaval of moving to Cheltenham and settling down to a new pattern of life with a baby, it was a few months before Margiad Evans managed to return to her writing. But in August 1951 she wrote to the ever-helpful Bryher: 'I'm writing a book. I've dedicated it to you'. Lindsay Drummond, who had published *The Old and the Young*, had gone bankrupt, but in the autumn her old friend Arthur Barker, who had published her first book, came to see her and had a look at the manuscript. He encouraged her to persevere with it, and in early December she was able to report to Bryher that the book was nearly finished and the contract with Arthur Barker signed. *A Ray of Darkness* appeared the following year.

It was based, as *Autobiography* had been, on her journals, but in this new book the journals are used in a very different way. In *Autobiography* very little new material had been added and turning the journals into book form had been largely a question of editing: omitting names, sentences or whole passages, and changing the emphasis, to ensure continuity of theme. But in *A Ray of Darkness*, although she used her journals to refresh her memory, and quotes passages from them verbatim, the book is written from the point of view of her present state, attempting to make sense of what has happened to her. She combines a factual and broadly chronological record of the onset of her illness and discovery of her pregnancy with a more abstract commentary on the significance of these events. Above all she asks why the epilepsy had struck her at that particular point in her life, and this leads her to a sustained meditation on the possible moral, spiritual, even religious significance of her illness. Once again Margiad Evans writes with little concern for conventional form and structure. The narrative shifts between the concrete and the abstract, which involves movement backwards and forwards in time; interpolated poems convey in a different register thoughts and feelings difficult to pin down in discursive prose, and some passages may seem to the reader to be of only peripheral relevance.

But the book is held together by two main forces. One is the firm chronological development over the book as a whole. The three sections into which she divided it are concerned with three major periods or states: the time leading up to her first fit, searching for signs of the impending change; the first fit and diagnosis of epilepsy, followed by the discovery of her pregnancy; and finally the birth of her child and her attempts to come to terms with these momentous events that had transformed her life for ever. The factual narrative of these events, now in the past, is subjected to commentary and analysis in the present time of writing the book, but overall the growth of understanding and acceptance of her condition is charted chronologically, hand-in-hand with the physical changes and external events, and this gives the book a strong internal logic.

The second force for cohesion is the author's own voice, which dominates the narrative. Some contemporary critics found this voice too dominant, and the British Epileptic Association felt that *A Ray of Darkness* was too self-centred an account to be of relevance to most epileptics. The fact that the fits were not a symptom of classic epilepsy but of physical damage meant that her account could be dismissed as atypical and irrelevant. She was hurt and upset by this unfair comment, for she had never suggested that her experience was universal or typical, nor did she attempt to speak for epileptics as a whole. She was vindicated, however, by an appreciative letter from Dr William Lennox, one of the foremost American specialists on epilepsy and other neurological disorders, who asked for permission to quote from her work in a forthcoming book of his own. Moreover many epileptics did read *A Ray of Darkness*, despite the negative attitude of the British Epilepsy Association, found comfort in it and wrote to tell her so.

The purpose of the book is twofold. First she wishes, as in

Autobiography, to provide a written account for others of a personal spiritual journey. As an individual she presents to others a possible model for understanding life in its spiritual as well as physical dimensions. In this respect it belongs within the same established literary tradition as the work of such writers as Jefferies and Thoreau, whom she deeply admired and uses in *A Ray of Darkness* as helps to guide her on the road to understanding. From a feminist point of view, her book can be seen as a forerunner of so many personal accounts of women's experience published in more recent decades, where the individual life is presented as an example of more universal experiences and where commentary on that life can help others to understand more fully their own situation in society. Such a narrative can therefore empower its readers to take greater control over their own lives. And although Margiad Evans's account of her epilepsy does not carry an overt political message as those more recent feminist works often do, it contains a clear social message in its plea for greater and more sympathetic public understanding of epilepsy.

This, then, is the second purpose of *A Ray of Darkness*: to explain and demystify the experience, to educate non-epileptics and remove their prejudices and misconceptions about the disease and its sufferers, as well as to reassure those who may, like her, have to come to terms with it in later life. She could not write as a scientific or medical expert, but she was a writer above all and felt she must make use of her literary confidence and skill to communicate these important messages. Her own strong voice conveying what has happened to her gives *A Ray of Darkness* immediacy and intimacy which draws the reader in, but it also gives authenticity to her account.

Above all, *A Ray of Darkness* is a brave and positive book. In the first pages she defines 'the story of my epilepsy' as 'an adventure of body and mind', and throughout she shows how her meditations took her beyond shock, distress and fear to calm insights into her condition and into life in general. At first the experience of having fits simply helped her to come to terms with the fear of death, for although she had long accepted the idea of her own mortality, as recently as March 1950 she had told Derek Savage 'I think that I am by nature afraid of death'. Unconsciousness in fits could teach very gently 'the probable darkness of death, and remove our fear of that descent' (*A Ray of Darkness*, 11). Looking back on *Autobiography*, she felt that its ending 'with its resignation to death, was not an end but my prophecy of what was to become of me and what was to grow intelligible to me' (p. 63). There she had first acknowledged God as Creator of the earth she loved, but that had been part of her sense of a continuity and oneness between all creation and herself as part of it, and now her relationship with nature had changed. Partly because her condition pushed her far more into human society and partly, no doubt, because she was no longer able to live in the country, she felt that her perception of the earth was 'more blurred. It is not so much *myself* as it was' (*A Ray of Darkness*, 156). This led her to feel she must look beyond the God of Creation to find a God of Love, a search that continued, but it also gave her what she described as a sense of separation. Again this may have had practical reasons, for she had been exiled from the Herefordshire countryside, her definition of herself had been undermined by the fits, and her illness gave her a sense of being different from others. Whatever the precise reasons, however, this feeling of separation led her on a journey of spiritual enquiry as she attempted to understand what was happening to her. The epilepsy might be of physical origin, but her suffering could have a different cause, she argued.

At first, therefore, she began to wonder whether the onset of the fits was a kind of punishment for some sin or failing. 'Is epilepsy a religious or a moral disease?' she asked (p. 97). If the disease, as she felt, was 'trying to tell me about myself', then perhaps it had not a physical but a spiritual or ethical origin (p. 173). This led her to the frightening conclusion that it could be a punishment for neglecting her Muse, for her 'creative laziness'. The idea of two separate sides to her personality was not new to her. The way she separated the artist Peggy Whistler and the writer Margiad Evans at the beginning of her career was symptomatic. In her journals and letters in the 1930s and 1940s she often refers to 'Margiad Evans' as the writer in her. 'Silence of M.E. continues but tonight she must be pulled awake', reads the entry for 3 March 1947. The writer was often at odds with the Peggy who kept house, gardened, loved gossip and read *The Woman's Weekly*. 'Miss Margiad Evans is an insufferable high brow', she told Gwyn Jones, 'but Mrs Peggy Williams likes horrors' (28 January 1946). After she was prescribed drugs to control her fits this sense of duality deepened, for now at the moment before unconsciousness she felt she was split into two or more entities. The experience of pregnancy added a further dimension, as she explored the unity and separateness of mother and child, an idea developed in the poem 'Gemini'. But this also recalls the 'twin-like' relationship between herself and her sister Nancy, noticed by friends when they were young and often reflected in her writings. An undated line-drawing sent to Bryher, likewise entitled 'Gemini', picks up both aspects of this theme of duality, for it shows two twin-like children as well as what appears to be a mother with her arms entwined around her child. It is striking that in the autumn and winter of 1949, months before she had her first fit, Margiad had repeatedly dreamed of herself in the body of her sister, shaken and contorted, grimacing and jerking.

She became increasingly convinced that she suffered from a split personality, seeing evidence for this in her increasing aversion to dividing things into two and in the fact that she was often struck by a fit when standing in a doorway. But if this were true, then all her visions of the unity of life and herself as part of it must be delusions. Her aim must now be to recover that lost sense of the unity of body, mind and soul. A possible solution that presented itself was the idea that the Ego, though one, attempted to be in many places at once. If so, then 'it was possible to be where I was and be elsewhere at the same time' and that this was 'spiritually symbolical of the One which is everywhere and the everywhere which is one' (*A Ray of Darkness*, 179). It was reaching this interpretation which allowed her to recover herself and so to start writing *A Ray of Darkness*, putting her gifts to the use of others. She had understood that two kinds of 'spiritual perfectings' were possible: the first, 'in one's own spirit' could lead only to 'immortal waking'; but the second, found in serving 'the necessities of others', led to rest, and rest seemed desirable. Rather than the exaltation of Bach, Blake or Emily Brontë, she now preferred the simpler model of the old countrywoman who had so often appeared in her writing and was now celebrated in a poem:

Here is her body.

Mary who was given to John.
There are her hands
drowned in buckets of water
with wrinkled nails
like shells in the sea:
These her arms
crucified on the red forest of the fire:
and her back
she gathered load by load
and bore
as Jesus bore his only tree.
These her eyes;
they saw God
in the necessities of others.

Her body shall sleep
she shall rest in the miles.
She shall not hear
the dry wood creak for the fire,
nor the cow low,
nor the clock stop,
nor the ripe fruit fall,
nor the garment tear.
She shall rest
For her feet are full of hills.
(*A Ray of Darkness*, 187-8)

At the end of *A Ray of Darkness* Margiad Evans had passed through what she described as a 'psychic phase' and was ready to be reintegrated into the world and human society. She recovered her former state of mind which, although it was a state of 'miserable impatience and mental velocity', allowed her to become a writer again. She was well aware that the book posed more questions than it answered: she was not telling, but *asking* a story, she noted (p. 162). It was also unfinished, for the story of her illness, her life and her death continued.

Eight
The Nightingale Silenced (1952-1958)

By the beginning of 1952 Margiad Evans had finished *A Ray of Darkness* and was adjusting to life in Cheltenham. Because of the risks if she had a fit when holding her daughter, and her own concern that Cassandra should not be distressed by seeing her fall unconscious, she had to have someone else with her as much as possible. While her husband was out a woman was paid to come in and help. Her love for her family made her condition even harder to bear at times: 'Alone it would be horrible but it wouldn't *matter*', she explained to Kate Roberts (10 August 1952). Understandably, she often felt that there was 'no time with a child to do anything', as she explained to Bryher (1 September 1952). She was also hampered by rheumatism and suffered a further setback when she was rushed into hospital with appendicitis in the spring. Yet she still found time to keep up her journals and to write further poetry and prose. That summer the magazine *John Bull* bought the rights to serialize *A Ray of Darkness*, and the extra money enabled the family to take a rare holiday in Cornwall. She also took advantage of the publicity the serialisation generated to persuade the BBC to let her broadcast a talk on epilepsy, for she was keen to make use of her gifts as a writer on behalf of other sufferers by helping to dispel the prevalent myths and prejudices about epilepsy. In 'A Silver Lining', broadcast on the BBC Light Programme (later Radio 2) in March 1953, she explained in simple terms what happened in an epileptic fit, as well as urging a more positive approach to the disorder.

Later that year Michael Williams was appointed to a teaching post at a church school at Hartfield in Sussex, and by November

Margiad and Cassandra had joined him. Their new home was a bungalow, the kind of house she had always scorned, and she did not take to the land. On an earlier visit to Sussex in February 1945 she had described it in her journal as 'a flat-coloured spoiled country – ugly as I'd expected'. Hartfield, she told Gwyn Jones was 'a pretty but rather dull place. And Sussex is just horrible. Never a hill' (21 January 1955). Now she was truly in exile. By this time, too, she was under increasingly strong medication and felt that she had energy but little concentration or direction. Her unpublished papers tend to confirm this, for those that can be dated in the early 1950s suggest that she lacked a single firm purpose in her writing. In her homesickness and in an attempt to salvage something from the lost past, she turned back once more to 'The Widower's Tale', completely rewriting the first sections, but it remained beyond her grasp and was abandoned in 1955. In the mid-1950s she did succeed, however, in finishing a play about Byron, based on his letters, as well as several short stories, but the quality was uneven and they were never published or broadcast. Both *The Welsh Review* and *Life and Letters*, which had published so much of her poetry and prose in the 1940s, had ceased publication and she was finding it harder to find a market for her work. She made another abortive attempt at Emily Brontë, wrote a short study of John Clare, and even embarked on a new novel. This last, 'The Churstons', perhaps inspired by her illness and her family's initial reaction to the news of her epilepsy, is a curious tale about a family of brothers and sisters who take a vow of celibacy because of the hereditary suicidal mania which has driven another sister to kill herself.

In this frenzied turning from one project to another work was often left unfinished or unrevised and Margiad's creative energy became dissipated. As her illness progressed and her drugs were changed or increased, her handwriting became less controlled and the urge to communicate ever stronger, as if her mind were running ahead of her failing body, trying to set ideas in writing before it was too late. Even when feeling tired and sick she felt impelled to record her life in her journals and her letters, constantly trying to make sense of her fate.

In the first months of 1954 her condition worsened and after a bad fit she was admitted on 5 May to the Burden Neurological Institute near Bristol, where Professor Golla had first diagnosed her condition. Apart from three weeks at home, she stayed in hospital under Professor Golla's supervision until 17 July. Later she was admitted to hospital in Tunbridge Wells, nearer Michael and Cassandra, and it was there that she wrote a further autobiographical work, which she described as 'a very mundane account' of her serious attacks and worsening condition. 'The Nightingale Silenced' is thus in some ways a sequel to *A Ray of Darkness*, but this time she saw her audience as medical professionals, not the general reader. Her awareness that before long her own literary and even physical voice would be silenced is symbolized by the image of the nightingale scared away by one of the nurses. She became increasingly disabled physically and feared the loss of her mental faculties too, so it is understandable that from now on much of her work has a nostalgic tone. It was that same year that she wrote one of her most lyrical farewells to her former life, a radio script called 'December Day', eventually broadcast in December 1956. 'Although my home is in Sussex now', it begins, 'it is about my old home in Llangarron, a border village in Herefordshire, that I want to talk tonight.' The script is an imaginative re-creation of a single day of her life there, busy with preparations for Christmas, and it evokes not only her own life there but the atmosphere of Llangarron itself and that Border region she had loved so well. A mixture of narrative, dialogue, poetry and song, it includes material drawn from her journals and a number of characters based on her neighbours and friends at Llangarron, such as Ellen and 'Peg-leg' Saunders. Although Margiad was homesick for Herefordshire, the finished script is more celebratory than nostalgic in spirit. As she came to feel her exile ever more keenly, however, memories of her past life became increasingly important to her and the tone of her work becomes more and more elegiac.

Often poetry seemed to be the most appropriate form of expression and she became increasingly prolific in this medium. In this she had some success too, for some were broadcast on the BBC's Third Programme in 1953 and others were published in periodicals and anthologies in the last five years of her life. One of these, 'In Memory of a Little God', published in *The Fortnightly* in 1954, picks up the devil figure who appears in the later versions of 'The Widower's Tale', and turns him into a kitchen god, a symbol of the magic and tradition lost with the modernization of country life:

> ...A god ran out of the dairy
> Aye, Black Blackie Gwyre is no longer –
> he has hidden where no book can find him.
> Turn the hay, turn the bowls, turn the brains all through Wales,
> take your torches through the mountains,
> Search Wales, no-one will remember him except the old, and the oldest
> blue-eyed woman joined to her knitting.
> ...None hears of him now: no woman
> rising to unpick a bad stocking by firelight
> finds the heel turned and empty the sops in the saucer:
> nor in the warm puffing dough the impress
> of a small black hand...

Her agent encouraged her to put together another collection and her second volume of poetry, *A Candle Ahead*, was published in 1956. It was her last book. The poems selected for this volume are again variable in both theme and quality. She returns to some of the themes of *Autobiography* and *Poems from Obscurity*, notably the relationship between herself, or humanity, and the natural world, and especially the problem of communicating in words an essentially non-verbal experience. This idea is found in poems such as 'Cherry Orchard in Bloom' and especially 'Nature and the Naturalist', where scientific analysis is seen as inadequate and a more intuitive form of observation is needed. However, many of the poems in *A Candle Ahead* reflect her present predicament. In some examples, as in *A Ray of Darkness*, she reviews her life in order to search for a pattern or meaning in it. 'The World', for example, traces her spiritual development from the turmoil she felt in her years as a young novelist, through the middle period of 'healthy quickness' and finally to her illness and need to come to terms with it. In the same poem she recalls how for a time she felt separated from that natural world with which she had previously felt such a strong sense of oneness: 'and so I thought of summer weather/but winter and myself I found together/leaning against the wind.' Again she considers the two kinds of mystical or spiritual perfection explored at the end of the previous book: 'and in mortality infinity I guessed/and in activity eternal rest'. The state in which she felt ideas pressing in on her from all sides is indicated by her 'whirling head', but once more she passes beyond that to discover a different kind of oneness:

> Only one track of meditation
> leads to and from the secret of creation,
> and in this singleness of thought
> I found the reconciliation that I sought.

There are further echoes of *A Ray of Darkness* in her poem 'On Milton's bust, at his cottage in Chalfont St Giles', where she not only pays tribute to Milton himself but links him with another of her heroes who had been much in her thoughts: 'Bach of poetry, those organ looks/outsoar their stone'.

The most important, recurring themes, however, are exile and approaching death. 'In the Post Office on pension morning' is a homage to the working poor among whom she had lived in the country, but it is also a reminder that old age is something she herself will not experience. Images from the natural world are often used to underline her plight. In 'The Forest' life is seen as a journey through the wood, but happiness in nature and solitude is short-lived and gives way to images of death and loss. The lark's song, joyous but brief, becomes a metaphor of transitory life in 'A Lark Sonnet', and trees become cages for the birds in 'Poem' (p. 11). Trees, traditionally an image of life, have increasingly negative connotations, and 'The Past' is dominated by the image of a huge tree,

> whose roots suck all the veins, whose shadow is
> dreadful: in whose low branches sit
> black bitter birds with claws, which croak and cry.
> That tree drops acid. Every drip is pain:
> that shade is tears.

There are more positive moments, however, for example in 'The Nightingale', where she returns to the image of the bird's song as a rare and precious source of joy.

The idea of loss recurs in various guises. In 'Sonnet Number 7' she laments the vanishing of her former revelation of the earth, here linked with the theme of exile: 'Why at one blow/I ask, the vision and the place where it could show?' The short 'Poem' (p. 18) seems to refer to her new surroundings in Sussex in the lines 'no field invites me to itself,/no gateway asks me home'. Loss is also the main theme of the sequence of sonnets with which the book ends, although these are ostensibly love poems, a new departure for Margiad Evans. Their object is not a real person, however, for the sequence is inspired by the unrealistic image of woman as love object in Thomas Hardy's novel, *The Well-Beloved*. As in *The Wooden Doctor* the lover creates an idealized image of the unresponsive object of love. Nevertheless, the poems could just as easily be read as a farewell to her old life and the Herefordshire countryside which had been her own 'well-beloved'. Many of these poems are elegies for herself, for example 'Oh Only One', which provides the title of the book:

> Owner of miracles I
> when I fade to my bed with a candle ahead
> of eternity:
> with a candle ahead I die.

At the end of the short story 'The Lost Fisherman' the candle-end glimpsed through Aunt Fran's window suggested a calm close to the day, but now the homely image of that light leads not to sleep but to death. Similarly in 'A Lark Sonnet' she awaits death which comes to her so soon, before old age:

> ...Eternity
> Is now my mood; and our name is enrolled
> with other dead names in the mason's fold
> of wrinkled stone. I had to die
> while youth was young enough for youth to end
> and old enough companion to befriend!

The sonnets, and a number of the other poems in strict metre and rhyme, are of very uneven quality. Margiad Evans seems constrained by the demands of their form and too often contorts syntax in order to fit the words into the scheme, so that even the superficial meaning is often obscure at the first few readings. Where she allows herself greater freedom, in 'Oh Only One!', for example, the effect is generally smoother and the poems communicate more effectively. But it is no coincidence that by far the most important and moving poem in the collection, 'To my sister Sian', is in free verse, allowing the words and their meaning to flow unhindered. This poem was written while Margiad Evans was in hospital and all too aware of the seriousness of her condition. Again it is an elegy for herself, and a review of her past life, but this time she concentrates on memories of the year at Benhall she shared with her sister Nancy and celebrates the close relationship they formed then. The importance of that shared past in the Border country is stressed by the quotation from *Autobiography* which precedes the poem: 'Do you remember, Sian? How dearly do you remember?'. But whereas in their original context those words celebrated the happy recovery of childhood vision through those memories, now they speak of loss and parting. The twin-like unity of the sisters, based on shared experiences, memories and affinity, will be broken, for death will soon separate them:

> Nature and Time are against us now:
> no more we leap up the river like salmon,
> nor dive through its fishy holes
> sliding along its summer corridor
> with all the water from Wales, nor tear it to silver
> shreds with our childish arms when it bolted our path for the day,
> nor wade wearing our bindings
> of string weed, white-flowering from our nakedness:
> nor lie in the hot yellow fields with the cows.

Since the bond between them had been so close, it is sad and strange to think that their deaths will be separate in time and space, especially when they could easily have died together in the course of their reckless play:

> We go home separately Sian.
> Strangest of all changes, that you have one door,
> I another! Dreamily I write to our childhood,
> sisters with a brotherly friendship, one loyal to both.
> There hang the black woods still with candles of daffodils
> lighting the draught of the wind, and our parted language

speaks to each of us of the keepers' cot in the brackeny corner
and the stream bed where the water had faded to rock –
Easily we keep our secrets now, for no-one cares
if we dare the red floods together, two little fools in the darkness
whose souls flew high above danger, whose bodies
death had a hundred times in its reach.

The poem recreates the timeless feel of that brief period when they formed their close relationship with each other and with the earth, sharing secrets, creating their own universe out of that part of the land they made their own. In her essay 'The Immortal Hospital', written a little later than this poem, she writes of 'a deep significance in the entity of every place around and in the farm, almost in every room. There was a secret. We were one in feeling it, but divided in the way we felt it.' Nothing that has happened to them since can change the memory of those days, and although the land itself may have undergone change since their childhood, in the remembering it is eternally the same. The land formed them and the land is as they saw it and named it. Land and sisters are identical, inseparable, and in memory both are unchanged:

Forever we
did not end, but passed over our paths,
I following you, dabbling our hands in the birds' nests,
darting through ghost walk and haunted graveyard
when the year was dead in the church tower.
We had one home together. That put us beyond all danger:
that set us forever, that and our unfathomable friendship with trees,
fields and horizons. Two children
solitary, pilgrimy, silent, inscrutably wishing
forever dallying with lostness, whether our choice was
through the jay woods, or over the mushroom mountains,
or the old cider orchards.

Our secrets
were eternal and will always be. Forever dallying
with lostness, at last we were lost and all paths
were the paths of our unforgettable double childhood.
All our secrets were one – secrecy.
The memory of what we kept secret is gone, but the secret is true.
All the places were us, we were all the places,

and the inscrutable innocent altars of nature.
I see two children slipping into a wood
speechlessly happy. Two lives have not changed it.
For our ways, our fields, our river, our lostness
were children. So we were our country.

She wrote no finer epitaph for herself.

The quality of her later uncollected and unpublished poems is again very variable, and they are often hard to understand fully, although their general meaning may be guessed. Many of them are deeply moving, however, for they reflect her sense of loss and knowledge of approaching death. She was still struggling with strict forms whose demands constricted her and tortured the syntax, but even the poems in free verse can be obscure. Perhaps this is partly because many of them are intuitive creations which came into her mind fully formed and underwent very little revision. Moreover, she had less energy and concentration, especially when her illness worsened or the drugs she had to take interfered with her thought processes. Certainly she was not always the best judge of her work in these last years, and often she knew it.

Her notebooks and correspondence in the years left to her give a moving, often harrowing account of her physical decline. They record her symptoms and feelings objectively, reflecting without self-pity her regret and concern for the effect of her condition on the lives of her husband and child. A further grant from the Royal Literary Fund and a Civil List pension allowed her to pay for assistance at home, although it was difficult to find anybody suitable locally. For a time Professor Golla held out hope that she might be cured, but she did not share his optimism. 'I cannot help feeling that my terrible enemy will overtake me', she wrote to Bryher in September 1954. At times she could scarcely believe what had happened to her: 'And is this the little girl of ten in the sunburnt field? Is this Peggy Whistler? Margiad Evans writing her novels and books?', she asked herself. 'No, it is some intensely unhappy creature ... who wishes everything undone. It has come to this: not a bud of life on the tree.' In January 1956 she began to be treated as an outpatient at the National Hospital for Nervous Diseases in London, under the care of Dr William Lennox. At the end of February she was admitted for a week so that Dr Lennox could perform an exploratory operation, and the truth was revealed: she was suffering from an inoperable brain tumour. Professor Golla had argued from the beginning that her fits were not classic epilepsy, but had been triggered by damage, but hitherto if a tumour had been suspected it had not been mentioned to her. Now she knew she could not live long. 'I have some desperate brain malady for which surgery can do nothing but nature sometimes does', she wrote to Gwyn Jones in 1957. 'This time next year I may be dead, non-compos or unable to move.' Original work became increasingly difficult but still she felt impelled to keep writing, for life without writing could not be life for her. She was touched by the support of her agent, David Higham, who visited her in hospital and talked to her intelligently in the midst of the noise of the ward and tried to have her moved to a private room.

In her last year she felt increasingly homesick for Herefordshire, and it was now that she wrote her most detailed evocation of childhood, 'The Immortal Hospital', explaining the comfort to be had from her memories:

> Hill Hall [Benhall] is the scene where I am always at my strongest, best loved and most enthralled. Hill Hall holds my youth. When lying awake, half teased by sleep or by my disorder or the horrible associations this disorder has brought ... at moments I can still be little Margiad at Hill Hall, if I try. Memory does not repose there ordinarily – a brooding mind seldom broods on happiness – but memory can be *sent back* by deliberate will. And once there, after the effort, an ethereal happiness permeates me and penetrates my restless mind. Some uninterrupted, unhurried, incorrupted peace the senses bring to me which seem to soothe my young untroubled self to sleep in my old body.

Soon revisiting Herefordshire in memory was not enough. At the end of December 1957 she told Bryher: 'I think I shall go home to live, if I can get there any how, as I have a longing to see the Black Mountains which sometime seem to hang from the sky like a rainstorm.'

Her thoughts also turned to the beginning of her career and to

Wales, to her stay in Pontllyfni and the writing of *Country Dance*. She decided to try reworking her first novel as a radio script and to her surprise and delight found that she could cope with the task. By late October 1957 she had a draft ready to send to the ever-faithful Gwyn Jones, through whose good offices the script was eventually broadcast, although not until two years after her death. The letter she sent him with the script gives a brave account of her condition: 'I can hardly walk, [and] though there is a distinct improvement mentally, and a fitful one in memory, there is a physical deterioration.' She ends on a characteristically defiant note: 'I had forty good years and crowded a lot in ... I won't be downed if there's anything left and if there isn't Cymru am byth.' She was consciously writing farewell letters to her friends, sending them her love in case each letter was to be the last. 'The world was very lovely', she wrote in one such letter to Bryher (19 December 1957). By the following January her fits were more frequent than ever. She could no longer walk and her sight was failing though her mind was still fairly clear.

At the end of January 1958 Gwyn Jones wrote to tell Margiad that *A Candle Ahead* was to receive an award from the Welsh Committee of the Arts Council and that this would be officially announced in March. She was just able to take in this good news that her last book had been honoured in Wales, but she was very ill and at the end of January had to be taken into the Kent and Sussex Hospital at Tunbridge Wells. Her mother, now aged eighty-two, had been helping to care for her for the last two years, and wrote to tell Gwyn Jones that Margiad would not be able to reply to his letter. She added: 'I do not think any one who loves her can hope for a prolongation of life. She is heavily drugged and though she speaks a little it is very confused and her mind is elsewhere most of the time. I do not think she wishes to be called back.' Margiad Evans died peacefully in hospital on the evening of 17 March. It was her forty-ninth birthday. Still in exile, she was buried three days later at St Mary's parish church, Hartfield. Her tombstone, as she would have wished, records the two sides of her life, for the inscription reads: 'To the memory of Margiad Evans, poet and novelist, wife of Michael Williams, mother of Cassandra'.

MARGIAD EVANS

* * *

During her lifetime, Margiad Evans was much admired as a writer, on both sides of the Border, although her books were never best-sellers by present-day standards. The practical difficulties of publishing during the Second World War and just afterwards undoubtedly limited the commercial success of her books at the very moment when she was producing her best work. Other important factors were her refusal to tailor her writing for a particular market or to bow to metropolitan fashions, and her unwillingness to spend more time in London making herself better known to the literary world. In Wales, in contrast, her standing was as high as ever in her last years and she has never lacked the enthusiastic support of the cognoscenti. But she is not a writer who can be easily pigeon-holed: she belonged to no recognizable school or movement, was no-one's disciple and had no obvious imitators. She simply wrote in her own way about what she knew, because she felt impelled to do so. It is true that Wales exerted a strong pull on her in her twenties and she was happy to be associated with journals such as *Wales* and *The Welsh Review*, where her work was published next to that of writers Welsh by birth, residence and even language and political commitment. But she did not wish to be labelled a Welsh writer, even when that might be to her advantage. She located herself and her writing firmly in the Border country, a choice which was understood and respected by her Welsh contemporaries but may in the long term have been to her disadvantage as far as London-orientated English critics are concerned.

One of the main reasons that the work of Margiad Evans has not received more attention since her untimely death, however, is that so much of her work has been out of print and remains so. Apart from *Country Dance, Autobiography* and *A Ray of Darkness*, even second-hand copies of her books are very difficult to find. Yet she is a richly rewarding writer who should be more widely read. Much of the work which filled the pages of periodicals and anthologies in the 1940s and 1950s is so much of its time that it is almost unreadable today except for its historical, documentary interest, and it is ironic that when Margiad Evans's *Autobiography* was published in 1943 she was criticized by reviewers for not bringing the war into the forefront. Yet her work, including *Autobiography*, has outlasted that of many of her contemporaries. It has never dated or lost its power, and her prose style remains as fresh and direct as ever.

Her work is rich in variety of themes and treatment and yet her own highly individual voice is unmistakable throughout, from the controlled, formal simplicity of *Country Dance* to the immediacy and passion of the three novels that followed, to the more thoughtful, lyrical qualities of *Autobiography* and *The Old and the Young*, which represent her most mature writing, and finally to the strange combination of the emotional, intellectual and spiritual in *A Ray of Darkness*. All of these elements can also be found in her poems, both published and unpublished, and although here the quality is not consistently high at its best her poetry, especially her free verse, can be extremely fine. And if virtually all her writing is in some senses a response to personal experience, that experience is not specific to an individual in a particular time and place but is always representative of the human condition. Hence even *A Ray of Darkness*, that very idiosyncratic account of the onset of her illness, has a timeless and universal value because its theme is the full realization of our impending mortality.

It could be argued, in fact, that all Margiad Evans's published work is concerned to a greater or lesser extent with the idea of death, but this does not make her a depressing writer. It is death which makes sense of life, and knowledge of it can and does enhance the individual's awareness and enjoyment of existence, whether it is Florence Dollbright in *Creed* gaining an enhanced and intensified awareness of life when she is dying but believes herself cured, or the narrator of *Autobiography* experiencing tremendous exaltation at being part of the cycle of nature which depends on death following and preceding life. Read in its entirety, the work of Margiad Evans is a celebration of the completeness of life, its dark and its light sides which are inseparable parts of its whole.

Other dualities are reflected in her work, notably the tension between the artist and writer in her, between Peggy Whistler and Margiad Evans, a tension resolved in *The Old and the Young*, where for the first time their identities are fused. But, more importantly, as a woman she experienced the archetypal conflict between her domestic and professional roles. This had been hinted at while she was at Springherne, failing to complete 'The Widower's Tale', but it was while she lived at Llangarron, where the constant physical labour left less time and energy for writing, that she became increasingly aware of the tension. The gregarious, cheerful housewife Mrs Peggy Williams gossiped with her friends and read *The Woman's Weekly*, whilst the austere, highbrow Miss Margiad Evans craved solitude and sat up writing till the early hours of the morning. At times she even writes of Margiad Evans as a muse figure, whose presence can be conjured up by a mood, a letter or a sudden glimpse of a place or person. Her brother-in-law, Bernard Williams, retains a clear image of the integration and yet separateness of the housewife and the writer. She often wrote kneeling down on the floor in front of the stove and he recalls seeing her there, bent over a manuscript she was working on 'as if bowing to the stove', the usual 'Craven A' cigarette 'sprouting from the side of her mouth.' She worked at her manuscript for over an hour, 'oblivious to all else', then suddenly got up to serve the hot broth that had been simmering on the stove. 'It was amazing how she could glide from one world to another.'

As a writer she was also aware of the potential conflict in the relationship between writer and reader. In novels such as *The Wooden Doctor* and *Creed* she made explicit play of this idea, prefiguring the concerns and techniques of far more recent writers. In *Autobiography* she developed these questions further, exploring in greater depth what is effectively a problem of communication. In both the novels and her journal-based prose she saw this as essentially a problem of 'translation', for the creative artist must struggle to express herself in ordinary language 'translated' from her own 'native language' in which the work is first formed. But if the writer's task is to convey inner thoughts in outer form, in order to communicate her meaning to the reader clearly, exactly and above all plainly, the starting point must be in the outer world. This is made clear in a key passage in her journal, written on 16 February 1947, in the middle of a very hard winter. She had been helping at the farm where her husband worked and whilst physically occupied she had been meditating on the act of writing and the relationship between the subjective and objective, inner and outer:

> With the hay on my head (I was carrying it to the calf shed) I was
> thinking of writing, and good writing. What I call inspired writ-
> ing. Pondering on the meaning of 'subjective' while the hay
> wriggled down my neck ... But looking around at the manure
> heaps and the snow stained with our mud as strawberries stain
> cream – and the black angry North and the birds, I thought if
> they are the objective then with me the objective and the subjec-
> tive are one. For these things are ['in my' deleted] mind – I
> almost seem to think them. And I wondered, is this common? To
> render outer things as inner ones, that seems to me the gist of the
> writing I like to read and to do.

It is this fusion that lies behind her finest writing. Her awareness of
the 'inner' aspects of the material world, the spiritual side of life,
makes Margiad Evans a profoundly mystic writer, but the fact that
her life was so deeply rooted in everyday reality prevents her writings from becoming obscure or heavy. The strong personality of the
writer as an individual and above all as a woman informs all her
work; taken together it forms a true autobiography, tracing her journey from childhood to maturity and decline. But if her own experience is often the starting point, her aim in the end was not simply to
enhance her own understanding of life and she was not interested in
popular success. 'I am not introspective', she stressed in her journal,
'and I don't want to *be* known but *make* known' (8 January 1946).
Her explicit attempts to achieve a greater understanding of the pattern of life and death, especially from *Autobiography* onwards, are
both highly personal and universal. Like Kate Roberts, whom she
admired as a 'classic writer', Margiad Evans sees the universal in
the particular, and knows that the universal is often best revealed by
close observation of the particular, in her case usually the
Herefordshire Border country and the people who lived there. Her
portrayal of life there is authentic and totally unromanticized, for
she had not only observed the primitive conditions but had lived in
them and knew the hardships at first hand. Yet because she had not
been born into the labouring class of a community like Llangarron,
and because as a writer, and a woman writer, she could never fully
belong to it, she was able to stand back a little and observe its

dynamics more dispassionately. Standing at the border between insider and outsider, she could make known the unsung lives of the people among whom she lived.

By now, nearly eighty years after she first saw Benhall and the river Wye, much of that countryside which first inspired her may have been lost or changed almost beyond recognition, as urban life with all its concomitants makes ever greater inroads. But if the landscape, material culture, social structures and even attitudes have altered, human lives and relationships are still much the same. It is that still-recognizable reality which has given the work of Margiad Evans the power to retain its accessibility and appeal, and allows it to be read on several levels. The qualities of her writings are not limited by that time and place in which they are so firmly rooted, and with repeated reading they yield more and more delights. Her best work, especially *Autobiography* and *The Old and the Young*, show her to be one of the finest prose writers in English this century, combining humanity, profound intelligence and intense feeling with an unusual clarity and richness of style. The work of Margiad Evans deserves to be more widely known and it is high time she was accorded the high status she has so fully earned.

Bibliography

Primary sources

The bulk of Margiad Evans's surviving personal and literary papers are held in the Department of Manuscripts and Records of the National Library of Wales, Aberystwyth. They comprise correspondence, journals and notebooks, drafts of published and unpublished prose and poetry, radio scripts, published and unpublished drawings, photographs and miscellaneous papers such as press cuttings. They were acquired in two groups, now Margiad Evans Manuscripts and NLW MSS 23357-74, 23577C; catalogue descriptions are available.

Other major archives held at the National Library include the letters from Margiad Evans among the Professor Gwyn Jones Papers, and the Margiad Evans Papers, which comprise materials for a biography compiled by W. Arnold Thorpe. Thorpe had barely started writing the biography itself before he died, but the archive he built up includes original letters from the writer's friends and relatives and transcripts of letters to them. Smaller groups of letters to various correspondents are scattered through other collections in the National Library of Wales and at other institutions in the British Isles, as well as in private hands.

Letters from Margiad Evans to Bryher, together with her Irish journal, a manuscript of *A Ray of Darkness*, and a number of drawings, are held at the Beinecke Rare Books Library, University of Yale.

Published work by Margiad Evans

Country Dance (London: Arthur Barker, 1932; repr. London: John

Calder, 1978)
The Wooden Doctor (Oxford: Blackwell, 1933)
Turf or Stone (Oxford: Blackwell, 1934)
Creed (Oxford: Blackwell, 1936)
Autobiography (Oxford: Blackwell, 1943; repr. 1952; revised ed., London: Calder & Boyars, 1974)
Poems from Obscurity (London: Andrew Dakers, 1947)
The Old and the Young (London: Lindsay Drummond, 1948; repr. Bridgend: Seren, 1998)
A Ray of Darkness (London: Arthur Barker, 1952; repr. London: John Calder, 1978)
A Candle Ahead (London: Chatto & Windus, 1956)

Uncollected prose

'The Little Red Umbrella', *New Statesman and Nation*, vol. 7, no. 168 (12 May 1934), 717-18.
'The Black House', *The Welsh Review*, vol. 1, no. 5 (June 1939), 242-6.
'Three Seas', *Life and Letters To-day*, vol. 46, no. 96 (August 1945), 90-7.
'Midsummer', *Life and Letters To-day*, vol. 55, no. 122 (October 1947), 70-4.
'Byron and Emily Brontë', *Life and Letters To-day*, vol. 57, no. 130 (June 1948), 193-216.
'The Man with the Hammer', *Life and Letters To-day*, vol. 59, no. 134 (October 1948), 11-27.
'A Party for the Nightingale', *The Welsh Review*, vol. 7, no. 4 (Winter 1948), 285-93.
'Arcadians and Barbarians or remarks on some English songs', *Life and Letters To-day*, vol. 61, no. 141 (May 1949), 110-26, and no. 142 (June 1949), 184-99.

Uncollected poems

'Poem', *Life and Letters Today*, vol. 58, no. 133 (September 1948), 226.
'The Initiate', *John O'London's Weekly*, vol. 62, no. 1529 (30 October 1953), 69.

BIBLIOGRAPHY

'In Memory of a little God', *The Fortnightly*, vol. 1053 (September 1954), 198-200.

'The Summer Wind', *The London Magazine*, vol. 4, no. 5 (May 1957), 63.

'Cure' and 'Poem', *New Poems 1957* (London: Michael Joseph, 1957), 44-5.

'To my Daughter', *New Poems 1958* (London: Michael Joseph, 1958), 36.

'Christmases', *The Cornhill Magazine*, vol. 170, no. 1018 (Winter 1958-9), 270.

Secondary sources

Moira Dearnley, *Margiad Evans* ('Writers of Wales' series, Cardiff: University of Wales Press, 1982)

P. J. Kavanagh, 'Margiad Evans', *The Listener* (11 Nov. 1971), 646-8.

Ceridwen Lloyd-Morgan, 'Portrait of a Border Writer', *Planet* 107 (October/November 1994), 45-54.

Idris Parry, 'Margiad Evans and Tendencies in European Literature', *Transactions of the Honourable Society of Cymmrodorion*, 1971, 224-36.

Idris Parry, *Speak Silence* (Manchester: Carcanet, 1988), 306-15 (reprinted in *PN Review*, vol. 15, no. 3 (1989), 29-32).

D.S. Savage, *The Withered Branch. Six Studies in the Modern Novel* (London: Eyre & Spottiswoode, 1950), 106-28.

Acknowledgements

I am most grateful to Cassandra E. Davis, daughter of Margiad Evans, for kind permission to quote from her mother's writings, and to both her and her father, Michael Williams, for access to manuscripts and other papers in their possession. Special thanks are due to Michael Williams who has been unfailingly kind and supportive, as has his brother, Bernard Williams. Others who have helped or encouraged me in various ways are Moira Dearnley, Professor Gwyn Jones, Dewi Roberts, Dr David Smith, Miss E.M. Snodgrass, John Powell Ward and especially Ned Thomas.

I also wish to acknowledge the award of a bursary from the Arts Council of Wales for the purpose of writing this book; the National Library of Wales kindly permitted me to take leave of absence. The National Library of Wales is also gratefully acknowledged for permission to reproduce all the photographs in the book, and that on the cover, with the exception of image number nine, which is reproduced by kind permission of Michael Williams.

Series Afterword

The Border country is that region between England and Wales which is upland and lowland, both and neither. Centuries ago kings and barons fought over these Marches without their national allegiance ever being settled. It is beautiful, gentle, intriguing, and often surprising. It displays majestic landscapes, which show a lot, and hide some more. People now walk it, poke into its cathedrals and bookshops, and fly over or hang-glide from its mountains, yet its mystery remains.

The subjects covered in the present series seem united by a particular kind of vision. Writers as diverse as Mary Webb, Dennis Potter and Thomas Traherne, painters and composers such as David Jones and Edward Elgar, and writers on the Welsh side such as Henry Vaughan and Arthur Machen, bear one imprint of the border woods, rivers, villages and hills. This vision is set in a special light, a cloudy, golden twilight so characteristic of the region. As you approach the border you feel it. Suddenly you are in that finally elusive terrain, looking from a bare height down on to a plain, or from the lower land up to a gap in the hills, and you want to explore it, maybe not to return.

There are more earthly aspects. From England the border meant romantic escape or colonial appropriation; from Wales it was roads to London, education or employment. Boundaries are necessarily political. Much is shared, yet different languages are spoken, in more than one sense. The series authors reflect the diversity of their subjects. They are specialists or academics; critics or biographers; poets or musicians themselves; or ordinary people with, however, an established reputation of writing imaginatively and directly about what moves them. They are of various ages, both sexes, Welsh and English, border people themselves or from further afield.

Margiad Evans is a sadly-neglected name in the twentieth-century list of Welsh writers in English. Admittedly her Welshness was a matter of adoption not birth; in fact she tended to insist that she wasn't Welsh, or English, but Border itself. Either way it is hard to see that *Autobiography* is anything other than a unique classic, for its observations of nature, rural work and own self reach the detail-saturation of Richard Jefferies himself, to whose work Margiad was devoted. It really should be available in a standard paperback edition. Many readers would speak as highly of *A Country Dance* and *A Ray of Darkness*, and the plain fact is that a complete edition of Margiad Evans's work is overdue. Ceridwen Lloyd-Morgan's immaculate and lucid interweaving of the life and work should do something to further this desirable outcome.

John Powell Ward

Index

Oliver, Percy, 44
Oxford, 14-15

Pontllyfni, 21-23, 33, 107, 139
Potacre, 78, 97, 99, 101, 111
Pouldu, 12-14, 22, 111
Pratt, Anna, 95
Pratt (*née* Whistler), Betty (ME's sister), 7, 33, 55, 67, 95, 100
Pratt, Dr William, 55, 67
Rampisham, 75
Rhys, Keidrych, 72
Roberts, Kate, 20, 21, 22, 87, 90, 106-109, 129, 143
Rosé, Jan, 99
Ross-on-Wye, 20, 62, 72, 75-76, 100, 101
Ross High School, 10
Royal Literary Fund, 122, 137

Salus, 20, 62
Savage, Derek, 34, 50, 54, 65-66, 81-82, 85, 88, 113, 114
Saunders, Mrs Ellen, 78, 97-98, 101, 131
Saunders, William, 'Peg-leg', 78, 131
Scudamore, Margaret, 78-79, 114
Smith, Miss, 75
Society of Authors, 114
Springherne Guest House, 70, 71-72, 74, 75
Stainer, Jacob, 99
Swinbrook Manor, 18, 43

Thoreau, Henry David, 88, 89, 115
Thorpe, W. Arnold, 21, 57, 58, 67, 79
Tower Hill, Llangarron, 99
Trevor, Eva, 79

Uxbridge, 7, 56

Walford, 71, 74
war (1914-18), 46
war (1939-45), 74, 76-82, 111, 141
Watts, Spencer, 18
Welsh language, 22-23, 32, 74

Whistler, Betty, see Pratt, Betty
Whistler, Godfrey James (ME's father), 7, 8, 10, 44-45, 50, 54, 66-67
Whistler, Henry Ratcliffe (ME's grandfather), 12
Whistler, James McNeill, 11
Whistler, Mrs Katherine Isabel (ME's mother), 7, 10, 44, 55, 67, 75-76, 77, 79, 139
Whistler, Nancy (ME's sister), 8-10, 14, 32-33, 43, 44, 45, 50, 55-56, 57-58, 64, 67-68, 70, 71, 74, 101-102, 114, 120, 127, 135-137
Whistler, Peggy Eileen, see Evans, Margiad
Whistler, Roger (ME's brother), 8, 11, 77, 79, 100
Williams, Alfred, 15
Williams, Bernard, 74, 101, 142
Williams, Cassandra Ellen (ME's daughter), 122-123, 129, 130, 131, 139
Williams, Hilda, see Howell, Hilda
Williams, Professor Ifor, 23
Williams, Michael (ME's husband), 7, 13, 14, 74, 77-81, 86, 87, 91, 93-101 *passim*, 111-112, 114-117, 119, 129-130, 131, 139
Williams, Reverend Thomas Mendus, 74, 79
The Woman's Weekly, 67, 126, 142
Wychwood School, 14
Wye, river, 7, 8

About the Author

Ceridwen Lloyd-Morgan was brought up in Caernarfonshire and studied at the universities of Oxford, Poitiers and Wales. Since 1981 she has been on the staff of the Department of Manuscripts and Records of the National Library of Wales, and has a special interest in the archives of writers and artists. She has published widely on the history of literature and the visual arts in Wales.

The Border Lines Series